# ANIMAL PLANET

# COMPLETE GUIDE TO
# DOG TRAINING

erything you need to know for a
appy, well-behaved dog

tfh

**JANICE BINIOK**

# COMPLETE GUIDE TO DOG TRAINING

Project Team
Editors: Mary E. Grangeia, Matthew Haviland, Jaclyn Ix
Indexer: Elizabeth Walker
Designer: Angela Stanford
Series Designer: Mary Ann Kahn

TFH Publications®
President/CEO: Glen S. Axelrod
Executive Vice President: Mark E. Johnson
Associate Publisher: Stephanie Fornino

Discovery Communications, Inc. Book Development Team: Marjorie Kaplan, President and General Manager, Animal Planet Media/Patrick Gates, President, Discovery Commerce/Elizabeth Bakacs, Vice President, Creative and Merchandising/Sue Perez-Jackson, Director, Licensing/Bridget Stoyko, Designer

TFH Publications, Inc.®
One TFH Plaza
Third and Union Avenues
Neptune City, NJ 07753

Printed and bound in China
16 17 18 19 20    1 3 5 7 9 8 6 4 2

Library of Congress Cataloging-in-Publication Data

Names: Biniok, Janice.
Title: Complete guide to dog training : everything you need to know for a happy, well-behaved dog / Janice Biniok.
Description: Neptune City, NJ : T.F.H. Publications, Inc., 2016. | Series: Animal planet complete guide | Includes bibliographical references and index.
Identifiers: LCCN 2015036653 | ISBN 9780793837434 (hardcover : alk. paper)
Subjects:  LCSH: Dogs--Training.
Classification: LCC SF431 .B445 2016 | DDC 636.7/0835--dc23
LC record available at https://lccn.loc.gov/2015036653

This book has been published with the intent to provide accurate and authoritative information in regard to the subject matter within. While every reasonable precaution has been taken in preparation of this book, the author and publisher expressly disclaim responsibility for any errors, omissions, or adverse effects arising from the use or application of the information contained herein. The techniques and suggestions are used at the reader's discretion and are not to be considered a substitute for veterinary care. If you suspect a medical problem consult your veterinarian.

Note: In the interest of concise writing, "he" is used when referring to puppies and dogs unless the text is specifically referring to females or males. "She" is used when referring to people. However, the information contained herein is equally applicable to both sexes.

*The Leader In Responsible Animal Care for Over 50 Years!*®
**www.tfh.com**

# PART ONE

## USING THIS

## GUIDE

# 1

# INTRODUCTION TO DOG TRAINING

**Y**our dog is born with all the basic outlines necessary to become a beautiful portrait of companionship and friendship, but it's up to you to add color and complete the picture. This comprehensive training guide offers all the tools you need to brighten, enhance, shade, and shape the relationship you have with your dog.

Dog training, after all, isn't just about controlling behavior. It's about learning how to communicate with your best friend so that you can create new ways to enjoy your time together. It's also about discovering your dog's talents and strengths to help him overcome his weaknesses. Through this process,

you will reinforce what you and your dog have in common as well as find ways to celebrate your differences. In short, dog training is about experiencing everything pet ownership has to offer and appreciating the whole picture.

Whatever your goals may be, whether you want to teach your dog a new activity, increase his command vocabulary, solve specific problem behaviors, or simply teach him a few new tricks, you'll find that the rewards of training go far beyond having a well-behaved

**Training creates a foundation for effective communication, which will strengthen the bond between you and your dog.**

pet. In teaching your canine pupil, you will no doubt learn many things yourself. It is truly a win–win experience for both of you.

## COMMUNICATION IS KEY

Training creates a foundation for effective communication, which any psychologist will tell you is the key to a healthy relationship. This doesn't just apply to human relationships; it also applies to the one you have with your dog. However, communication is a little more difficult with another species. You and your dog are much like two foreigners who have befriended each other on an exotic vacation. You probably manage to find ways to interact despite your language differences, but imagine how much better it would be if you could teach your dog human language and perhaps learn a little bit of canine language yourself. That's what training can do for you!

Does your dog have difficulty understanding what you want? Do you sometimes become bewildered, wondering why your training techniques don't seem to work? Maybe you've even been harboring the secret suspicion that your dog got the short end of the stick in canine intelligence. More than likely, though, your problems are simply due to communication barriers.

Dogs may not be capable of learning the entire human language, but they are definitely capable of learning enough of it to become excellent companions. If your dog is not the perfect canine partner you think he should be, this book can help you overcome common challenges to becoming better buddies. Dogs naturally

have a desire to please their owners, so being able to express your desires in a way they can understand is the first step toward having more obedient, well-mannered members of the family.

Obviously, communication barriers create plenty of frustrations for dogs as well. When a pet does not understand what is expected of him, when he is berated for behaviors that come naturally to him, or when he cannot communicate that he needs something, he may act out through disobedience or destructiveness. Life in a human world is a lot easier for a dog who is taught appropriate behavior in terms he can understand. Training will help provide him with a sense of security, comfort, and belonging. And just like humans who communicate effectively and frequently with each other, you and your dog may even begin to think alike. Both of you will be able to reap the rewards of a more enjoyable relationship. Isn't that why you got a pet in the first place—to enrich your life?

## WHY TRAIN YOUR DOG?

Being able to communicate with your dog might be reason enough to invest the time and effort needed to train him, but there are plenty of other benefits as well. Teaching him various commands can help keep him safe when he may not know any better. It's a scary world out there filled with all kinds of hazards— traffic, wild animals, toxic substances— and dogs, unfortunately, are not always cognizant of the dangers. Furthermore, training your dog can make life easier for everyone who comes into contact with him. Neighbors, guests, and even strangers you meet on the street will appreciate a pet who has been taught good manners, and it's up to you to teach him how to function in all situations. When you succeed in this, you contribute to the greatest benefit of all: the acceptance of canines as valuable members of the human community.

## Think Like a Dog

The first step to successfully training your dog is to learn each other's language. Good communication leads to better understanding. Better understanding leads to more appreciation. And when you truly understand and appreciate your dog, you may just realize that teaching him command words has actually caused you to speak less because you'll say what you mean and mean what you say. You will have shed all the unnecessary, extraneous gibberish for the essential gold nuggets of vocal connection. And the more you communicate with your dog, the more you will become mentally connected as well. Like a long-time married couple who tends to finish each other's sentences, you will begin to think like your dog and your dog will think like you, to the point that words may not be necessary at all.

## HOW MANY COMMANDS CAN A DOG LEARN?

Dogs can be taught an incredible number of commands as long as they have the opportunity to learn them in a consistent, positive way. In his book, *The Intelligence of Dogs*, Stanley Coren mentions that his dogs knew at least 60 different words and phrases—and this was not the result of a concerted effort to teach them a large vocabulary. They learned many of these words simply by hearing them frequently, at the appropriate times, throughout the course of their daily lives. According to Coren, an average dog may actually be capable of learning up to 165 words.

In the sport of canine musical freestyle, dogs are required to learn more verbal commands than in any other sport. Patie Ventre, the president and founder of the World Canine Freestyle Organization (WCFO), revealed that her dog, Dancer, had a vocabulary of at least 70 commands. This did not include words and commands recognized outside of the sport. Other WCFO members who responded to an inquiry indicated their dogs knew between 40 and 60 commands related to canine musical freestyle. They, no doubt, knew words and commands well in excess of these numbers if all other communications were considered.

So as you're deciding what and how much to teach your dog, you need not limit yourself to a specific number of commands fearing you'll reach his full capacity. Do you think that teaching him all 101 commands in this book is too lofty a goal? Actually, it isn't unrealistic should you desire to achieve it. In fact, if you have an exceptionally brilliant canine, this book may be no more than a primer!

A report published in the journal *Science* ("Word Learning in a Domestic Dog: Evidence of 'Fast Mapping,'" June 11, 2004) discussed experiments with a Border Collie named Rico who learned at least 200 words. And if you think that's impressive, another Border Collie, Chaser, took over the title of "canine king of communication" when a 2010 study at Wofford College in South Carolina revealed his ability to remember more than 1,000 words!

So if dogs are capable of learning that many words and commands, why do so many have such limited vocabularies? The answer is twofold. First, a dog's ability to learn and respond to human language has been woefully neglected and underdeveloped throughout history. Perhaps humankind's long-held belief that beings besides ourselves could not possibly understand language led us never to explore an animal's true potential. Second, many owners simply do not know how to teach their dogs to understand them. Typical canine exposure to language may consist of yelling, cajoling, scolding, pleading, babbling, jabbering, sweet talk, baby talk, and cute little kissy noises—none of which help a dog learn to understand anyone.

Your dog may have more learning potential than you realize; however, it doesn't accomplish much to teach him a bunch of commands just to prove how smart he is. That's why this training guide is particularly valuable for advancing his education in more meaningful ways. Choose the commands and words that can benefit your living situation, add fun to your leisure activities, or contribute to your particular human–canine relationship.

## Verbal Commands Versus Hand Signals and Body Cues

Use of verbal commands tends to be the norm in dog training, but what about hand signals and body language? Dogs and humans actually communicate using the same tools: vocalization, body language, and behavior. Humans have just become so good at verbal interaction that they tend to rely on it more than dogs do, but that doesn't mean vocalizations aren't important to dogs.

In some instances, hand signals or body cues are convenient and easy to use, but there are also advantages to having a verbal form of every command. For example, have you ever tried telling your dog to move out of the way using hand signals when you're carrying an armful of groceries? As you can see, it's always good to have a "name" or command word for everything you teach your dog. His hearing is amazingly acute, and his sensitivity to voice inflections is profound. We would be overlooking a valuable resource if we ignored a dog's capacity for verbal understanding.

# 2

# HOW TO USE THIS TRAINING GUIDE

The *Complete Guide to Dog Training* isn't your typical training manual. It incorporates skills from a variety of disciplines, explores the multiple uses of each, and brings them all together into one easy-to-use resource. In addition to covering the basic principles of dog training, this book includes instructions that are written and organized like a reference book, with commands listed in alphabetical order. This may very well be the first and last dog training book you'll ever need!

But just like any other reference material, how much you get out of this book will depend on how you use it. You probably wouldn't read a dictionary or encyclopedia from cover to cover, and you may not want to read this book that way either. A couple of conditions must exist to get the most benefit out of this type of resource: You need to know how to locate the information you seek, and you need to know how to apply that information to achieve the results you desire.

To that end, the *Complete Guide to Dog Training* is conveniently organized into three carefully designed sections. Part One explains how to best use this book to meet your particular goals. Part Two is devoted to essential training concepts and

**Basic training teaches your dog how to successfully adjust to life in your family's household.**

language practices that will maximize the effectiveness of the training instructions provided in the last section, Part Three. In this section, training skills are presented in separate categories in individual chapters, making it easy for you to locate the type of commands that interest you. For example, if you want to learn obedience training, you can choose from a number of basic commands outlined in Chapter 7. If you want to teach your dog some fun tricks, you can find step-by-step instructions in Chapter 12. Chapter 6 will steer you toward skills that will enable you to solve problem behaviors, which perhaps may benefit you and your dog the most.

It is not necessary to read Part Two in its entirety before jumping into the various command training instructions in Part Three, but doing so may significantly improve your results.

## ABOUT PART TWO: TRAINING BASICS

There are two things that turn good trainers into great ones: knowledge and experience. The *Complete Guide to Dog Training* is more than a how-to book: It includes the what's, where's, and why's of dog training. Along with learning how to teach commands, it also includes a foundation in canine psychology that will help you to understand what may be behind some of the things your pet does. How can you work with your dog's natural instincts and personality traits to influence his behavior in the way you would like? Do you really need to be your dog's leader? Or should you be his best friend?

The section on positive training in Chapter 3 illustrates how you can teach your dog using resistance-free methods. It explains the basics behind behavior shaping, and it outlines the concepts necessary for you to have a lasting, rather than temporary, impact on his behavior. But these methods offer more than effective training techniques. They also contribute to enjoyable experiences for both you and your dog, and they result in greater communication and ultimately a closer bond between you.

The most important chapter in Part Two—and perhaps the single most important chapter in this entire book—is Chapter 4: Communicating With Your Dog. This chapter delves even further into essential communication skills. You can't train if you can't teach, and you can't teach if you can't communicate. If you've ever had a physics or calculus professor who knew his subject well but couldn't communicate it, you know that knowledge is worthless if you can't make it understandable to others. Although some of the chapters in this book may not pertain to your situation, Chapter 4 pertains to everyone. You need to master this system of communication to teach your dog any of the training commands presented in Part Three.

Even though you need to teach your dog to understand basic commands, the emphasis is on *you* to become proficient in delivering them. It will take a conscious effort and lots of practice for these cues to become a habit for you, but the more consistently and frequently you use them, the faster your dog will learn what they mean and how to respond to them.

Successful training basically consists of letting your dog know what you want him to do, and more importantly, what you don't want him to do. So it's very important for you and your dog to learn and apply a reliable system of communication. It will be the foundation of your dog's education, whether he masters only elementary skills or more advanced ones.

With every skill you teach your dog, you'll learn something new yourself and gain more confidence in your training ability. Wherever possible, alternative methods are offered, allowing you to customize training sessions in order to meet your dog's unique needs. In the

Dogs naturally have a desire to please their owners, so being able to express your desires in a way your dog can understand is the first step toward helping him become a more obedient, well-mannered companion.

process, you'll discover your own training talents and what works best for you.

Dog training is much like any other type of activity in which you choose to participate—the better you get at it, the more you will enjoy it. As much fun as you'll have working with your canine best friend, the impact of your efforts will go farther and deeper than you realize. Although basic training in areas such as socialization, crate training, and housetraining, along with tips on solving problem behaviors, are very important for teaching your dog how to adjust to life within your family household, almost every command in this resource will help him understand a little more about the rules and expectations of human society. Most importantly, you'll learn how to acknowledge and appreciate him for what he is: a dog. Such acceptance is, without a doubt, the foundation of unconditional love.

## ABOUT PART THREE: TRAINING COMMANDS

Each training command in the *Complete Guide to Dog Training* includes alternative command words and several headings that define the scope of each command. These headings make it easy for you to choose the appropriate commands for your purposes because you can't always rely on the face value of words. For instance, the definition of *gee* has nothing to do with an expression of enthusiasm or surprise, and the definition of *hike* has no relation to a long walk. Command headings include: Description, Uses, Prerequisites, and Training Techniques.

## Alternative Commands

Alternative command words appear on the same line as the main command word; they are enclosed in parentheses after the word "also." They also appear in the Index, so if you cannot find a command among the main command word listings, you can locate it there.

Alternative commands are a valuable feature of the *Complete Guide to Dog Training* because there are several reasons why you may want to choose

an alternative. Most importantly, you will have greater success teaching your dog a new command if it does not sound too much like one he already knows. For instance, the *by me* and *behind*

## When Can We Start?

Any puppy old enough to go home with you (8 to 12 weeks of age) is old enough to train. However, always keep in mind that young puppies require a gentle hand and a lot of repetition to absorb their lessons. To begin, you can work on name recognition so that your pup will learn to pay attention when you say his name. Focus on simple obedience commands to give him a foundation for higher education. Then, as he matures, you can tackle more complicated and difficult skills. The speed at which your pup advances depends on his individual capabilities as well as your skill in training. Contrary to the familiar adage that an old dog can't learn new tricks, even senior canines can expand their command repertoire. Much like training a young puppy, training a senior may require extra patience and repetition. When you are realistic in your expectations and keep your training age appropriate, you will see the best results for your efforts.

*me* commands sound so similar that your dog is likely to get them confused, especially if you use them in similar situations. To prevent this, it's best to replace one of your command words with an alternative command word that sounds very different. You may also be tempted to use the same word for two different skills. *Back* can instruct your dog to either walk backward or to get in the back of your car. Decide on only one use for a command word and choose an alternative word for the other behavior. To communicate most effectively, it's important to abide by the rule "one word, one meaning."

Alternative command words don't exist solely to solve communication discrepancies. If you like an alternative command better than a main command word, go ahead and use it. Choose words that come to mind easily, because once your dog has acquired a sizeable command vocabulary, it can be challenging to remember all the commands he knows. In fact, it helps to make a list of the commands you've

Even though you need to teach your dog to understand basic commands, the emphasis is on *you* to become proficient in delivering them.

taught him so that you can practice and reinforce them regularly. If you neglect to do this, he may eventually forget some of his schooling.

Also, remember that once you choose a word for a command, you need to stick with it. Changing your mind about which words you use will only confuse your dog and hamper his training. In line with being consistent in your usage, you also need to be consistent in *how* you use words. Be sure to speak each command clearly and use the same tone of voice each time you utter it. Your dog responds as much to your intonation as he does to pronunciation.

## Categories
Commands fall into several categories, depending on the type of dog training they represent, and each category is conveniently packaged into its own chapter in this book.

> Obedience commands will give you control over your dog's behavior, both at home and in public.

It's important to know the scope of each category so that you can find the commands that are most important to you. What kinds of canine behaviors do you seek to manage? What kinds of activities do you want to enjoy with your dog? And don't forget to think ahead— how far do you want to go with your dog's training? The various categories will help you locate and focus on those areas that will benefit you and your dog the most.

For example, if your dog is lacking instruction in basic obedience, you'll find all the commands you need in Chapter 7. Obedience commands will give you basic control over your dog's behavior, both at home and in public. They also serve as a foundation for any advanced training you may wish to pursue. For these reasons, this chapter is a good place to start if you have just acquired a dog or you are new to training.

Chapter 8: Handling Commands is useful if you want a dog who tolerates being touched or physically handled. This is especially important for dogs who require intensive grooming, but it also comes in handy for physical exams at the vet's office. Even therapy dogs will benefit by learning some of these skills because they must tolerate being touched and petted.

Chapter 9 discusses household manners. It includes commands and communication that can make it easy to live with your dog. You can imagine that a pet without manners is just as annoying as a child without manners. When company comes, you can be proud of your dog's behavior because he will know his limits and boundaries.

If you want to pursue off-leash skills, work with the commands in Chapter 10. They will help you gain control of your dog in myriad situations outside of the home and make walking him and participating in public activities safe and enjoyable. Many of these skills are useful for a variety of competitive canine sports as well.

Last, don't forget to nurture your dog's fun side by choosing some commands from Chapters 11 and 12, which provide everything you need to know to participate in play and games you can both enjoy. Even though these commands may seem frivolous, they have practical applications beyond their

## Making the Team

Today, there are more competitive sports and activities to enjoy with your dog than ever before, and new ones are created all the time. From traditional obedience trials to more recent sports like canine musical freestyle and nose work, there is something that appeals to almost any type of canine talent. If you already have a specific activity in mind to try with your dog, remember that his training will involve more than learning the necessary skills for competition. Public events also require manners and social skills. Consider working with him on basic training (Chapter 5), as well as teaching him as many obedience commands as possible (Chapter 7). And of course, dogs who participate in any type of group activity should be healthy and up to date on their vaccinations. With proper care and training, you and your dog can safely and successfully participate in the activities you enjoy the most.

entertainment value. There is no such thing as a useless command! Teaching your dog *jump* may come in handy when you need him to traverse a mud puddle, or teaching him *spin* is a good way to get him to wipe his feet on the rug when he comes into the house.

At the very least, the time you devote to training will allow you to build a strong bond with your canine buddy. It will help you communicate more effectively, and it will boost both his confidence and yours. So when it comes to choosing commands, don't be afraid to think outside the categorical box, so to speak. Be creative; the possibilities are endless!

## Descriptions

Each command entry includes a description similar to one you might find in a dictionary. It describes what the command will accomplish and the reaction your dog is expected to have to it. These descriptions are necessarily brief and do not represent a command's full potential. They are intended to provide a visual picture of what the command will mean to your dog. Although a command will represent only one action or behavior

> A dog will feel more secure, confident, and content when he is given boundaries for his behavior.

to your dog, it may have many different meanings for you, depending on how you use it. As such, you will find the best indicator of a command's value in the Uses section.

## Uses

This heading provides suggestions for both traditional and alternative uses for a command. Just as a dictionary will give the linguistic origin of a word (e.g., Latin, Greek, or French), this heading may also note a command's origin in dog training. Most command words come from disciplines such as obedience, agility, herding, sled dog training, or canine musical freestyle.

Never assume that the uses for a specific command are obvious. Many have multiple practical applications, some of which you may not have considered. Study the possible functions that a command may be able to perform for you, and don't think that it has to be limited to one use. Once your dog has learned a particular command, you may use it in as many different situations as you like.

Your dog will need to know some preliminary skills, like *sit* and *stay*, before he is able to master more difficult commands.

In fact, using a command in more than one context offers several advantages. For one, it gives you lots of opportunities to apply it, which helps your dog practice the skill and keep it intact. Just like people, dogs tend to forget their education if they never use what they have learned. It's also a great way to "proof" your dog so that he will learn to understand and respond to the command in any location and under any circumstance.

This book includes the most common uses for commands, but you may also come up with a few of your own. Evaluate your own needs and decide how you can use a command to benefit yourself or others.

## Prerequisites

Each word represents a particular pattern of behavior you expect from your dog. Some behaviors are obviously more complicated than others, and so they require more training steps. Your dog may need to know some preliminary skills before he is able to master more difficult behaviors. For this reason,

> Your dog's intelligence, temperament, and age will affect his response to various training methods.

each word entry includes a Prerequisites heading that lists the commands or skills he must know in advance.

Think of these prerequisites as preliminary training steps. If your dog does not know some of them, look them up and teach them first. Attempting to teach your dog a skill without first teaching him the required prerequisites may ultimately confuse and frustrate him. At the very least, he will not develop a very good perception of training.

## Training Techniques

The training techniques covered in this book consist of numbered instructions that will take you step by step through the training process. They are all based on positive methods. (The concepts and components of positive dog training are discussed in Part Two: Training Basics.)

Consider your dog's physical makeup when training. A long-backed dog, for example, may have trouble with some commands.

As nice as it would be to plug these instructions into your dog and download them at the press of a button, dogs are not computers. Your particular pet's intelligence, temperament, and age will affect his response to various training methods, which is why the instructions offer alternatives whenever possible. Dogs learn in different ways, and they also have their own strengths and weaknesses when it comes to "subject matter." Your dog may be especially talented in learning and executing some commands, but he may have considerable difficulty learning others. Work with his natural abilities.

For example, if your dog has absolutely no interest in the game of fetch, it may be unproductive to teach him the *fetch* command. Also, consider his conformation and physical condition when you choose commands. It may be difficult or uncomfortable for a long-backed dog to learn the *beg* command, for example. Jumping, rolling, crawling, and running require some amount of exertion. Is your dog up for it?

If you notice that your dog frequently declines to obey a command, even though he knows it well and is generally obedient, it may be because he really doesn't enjoy doing that particular skill. Unless it is a basic obedience command or a command you need to manage behavior, remember that there are plenty of other things you can teach. It's rarely necessary to force your dog to do something he really doesn't feel comfortable doing.

Although many of the training techniques featured in this book include the use of food rewards for positive reinforcement or for luring your dog into a desired behavior, there are many that do not. Whenever possible, nonfood training methods are preferred because they help give greater value to other types of rewards, such as praise and attention.

Promoting a higher value for these types of rewards helps to strengthen a dog's will to please and contributes to obedience and confidence. Food rewards are a valuable training tool, but just as you wouldn't use a hammer on a thumbtack, they really aren't necessary to teach many of the commands in Part Three.

Regardless of the techniques you choose to use, remember that training should always be a fun activity. If you realize that you and your dog are not enjoying what you're doing, it's time to end your training session until you can invoke a more cheerful frame of mind. Always end sessions on a positive note by asking your dog to perform a skill he knows well, and then reward him. This will help restore his confidence so that you can both look forward to working together again.

PART TWO

TRAINING

BASICS

# 3

# DOG TRAINING ESSENTIALS

If training techniques provide the step-by-step recipes for having a well-behaved dog, then the concepts that embody those techniques are the ingredients. No matter how well you follow any recipe, things may not turn out the way you expect if you don't use the right ingredients. You can certainly take your chances and guess which ones to use and in what amounts to apply them. If you are an experienced cook, er, dog trainer, you may indeed already have a good idea of how to achieve desirable results. And that is why *Complete Guide to Dog Training* is appropriate for trainers of every level.

You don't necessarily need to read all the training essentials to use this book. If you have a firm grasp of the basics, go ahead and jump right into the instructions for the commands you wish to teach. However, the information in this section can strengthen your dog training skills if you are a beginner, and it can provide a refresher course if you already have some experience.

Although it takes a certain amount of mastery in the skills needed to train your dog successfully, there are tools, equipment, and supplies that can make the job easier. Some of them, like a leash and treats, are staples in training. Others are more specific to the type of command or behavior you want

**Every dog needs a confident leader he can respect and rely on for guidance and protection.**

to teach. Understanding the purpose of each, and learning how to use them appropriately, will help you communicate more effectively with your canine pupil. The various supplies and training aids are discussed later in this chapter.

## CANINE LEADERSHIP

One of the most important concepts in dog training is leadership. Here's why you need to be a trusted leader:

- Some dogs are rather independent-minded and may resist listening to their owners in favor of pleasing themselves. If you want an obedient, well-mannered pet, you need to make it clear to him that you're in charge.
- Some dogs are shy or insecure. As such, they need a firm leader they can trust.

- Some dogs have very powerful instincts. Prey drive, which is the compulsion to chase things that move, can be exceptionally strong in some breeds, and the only reason such a dog will listen to his owner rather than his own instincts is because he knows you're in charge.

In any of these cases, a lack of leadership will result in disobedience or even serious problem behaviors.

If you are not consistent in your teaching, discipline, and expectations, you cannot expect your dog to be consistent in his obedience.

### The Importance of Confident Guidance

When you consider the kind of attitude it will take to guide your dog's behavior,

think about the kind of leader who would earn your own respect. Would you appreciate the subjection of a tyrant or the confident guidance of someone who loves you? In this respect, a leadership role with your dog should be similar to that of a parent toward a child. You need to be firm, fair, trustworthy, and reliable. Express love without coddling and tough love without cruelty.

Always remember that your dog's behavior is directly related to *your* behavior. If you are not consistent in your teaching and expectations, you cannot expect your dog to be consistent in his obedience. If you harbor unstable emotions, like anger or mood swings, your dog will harbor a lack of trust and respect. Be conscious of your own behavior and how it affects your dog.

> Power commands, like *heel*, reinforce and support your leadership status with a dog by allowing you to control his movement and resources.

## POWER COMMANDS

Power commands are those that specifically allow you to control movement and resources—something that only a person in a leadership position can do. Some of these commands put you in a "first" position, and some help to nurture the will to please.

Commands like *stay*, *wait*, and *this way* control your dog's movement and direction. Commands like *off* and *move* require your dog to yield his resources (space) to you. *Back off* allows you to be the first to greet arriving guests, and *good* provides your dog with the pat on the back he needs to continue to seek your approval.

Power commands are identified as such under the Uses heading that is found under every command word. Consider teaching your dog some or all of the following power commands (you can look them up in the Index to locate the training instructions for them in this book):

- *back off*
- *be close*
- *behind me*
- *drop it*
- *gee*
- *good*
- *go on*
- *haw*
- *heel*
- *move*
- *naughty*
- *off*
- *on by*
- *out*
- *stay*
- *this way*
- *wait*
- *wait up*
- *walk on*

## POSITIVE TRAINING

Positive dog training earned its name from its use of positive reinforcement but also from the standpoint that it is a resistance-free type of training. You do not need to physically force your dog to do anything. This isn't to say that positive methods don't involve any form of consequence. Balanced training requires both positive reinforcements to encourage repetition of desired

## Kids Training Dogs

Kids and dogs make great companions for each other, and dog training is an activity that can create an exceptionally strong bond between them. Trick training is especially appealing to children because it is fun and entertaining, and it can be a valuable learning experience for all involved. But as with any type of child–animal interaction, dog training requires adult guidance. For safety and success, parents must make sure that all necessary skills are within the child's ability to teach and that complicated commands requiring prerequisites and difficult instructions are avoided. Supervision is also required to make sure the child handles and treats the dog appropriately. A large animal will be difficult for a child to control, so it may be best to give her the role of "assistant trainer," which will still enable her to learn valuable pet handling skills that will last a lifetime.

behaviors and negative reinforcements to discourage the repetition of undesired behaviors.

Fortunately, positive dog training relies on contemporary knowledge of canine psychology, which means it employs consequences that are psychological rather than physical in nature. In addition to being a kinder way to teach dogs, it provides quick results and enjoyable learning experiences for both dogs and owners. It also creates strong bonds between them. It's obvious why these methods have become so popular!

## Positive Reinforcement

Positive reinforcement may consist of giving your dog something he values, such as treats, praise, petting, playtime, or freedom. It may also take less conspicuous forms as well. For example, when your dog stands patiently while you clip on his leash, his reward is that he gets to go for a walk. When he shows good manners and waits for an invitation before he jumps into your lap, his reward is the invitation. Such rewards encourage your dog to repeat the behaviors you want.

The use of food rewards as positive reinforcement has become quite prevalent in modern dog training, and it's easy to see why. Food is a very powerful motivator for most canines. It keeps them interested,

**Positive reinforcement— rewarding your dog when he does something right—is a very effective way to get the behavior you want.**

focused, and eager to learn. It has a positive effect on a dog's attitude, which helps to keep training sessions fun and productive. It is also an ideal lure that makes it possible to train behaviors that would otherwise be difficult to teach. But food rewards do have their limitations.

Some dogs trained with food may refuse to obey a learned command unless they receive a food reward. Though this is sometimes referred to as "food dependence," the situation has more to do with respect than food. Most dogs are capable of understanding the difference between earning rewards during training sessions and obeying commands out of respect in everyday situations. You must make it clear to your dog that you *expect* compliance to your commands even when you do not have food to offer. Be prepared to enforce learned commands in the absence of food.

Food rewards are not necessary or even desirable in order to teach your dog many of the skills in this book. In cases where they may help expedite the training process, they have been included in the training techniques for a command. In other cases, the instructions may include nonfood training techniques. Food rewards are a tool, so use them judiciously and appropriately.

When you do use food rewards, take steps to avoid spoiling your dog's balanced diet or contributing to his weight gain. Always use very small tidbits (about

the size of the tip of your little finger), and measure the amount of treats prior to each training session.

Food is a powerful motivator for most dogs. It keeps them interested, focused, and eager to learn.

You may also need to adjust the amount of food you feed your dog at mealtimes to compensate for his consumption of treats. Treats that are easy to digest and devoid of preservatives and additives are healthier, but of course, you need to choose something your dog likes. Choose a food reward that motivates him without getting him overly excited.

## Fading Food Rewards

It's important to determine which commands will require continual food rewards (such as tricks for treats) and which ones you will eventually want your dog to perform without the incentive of food (such as obedience commands). For the latter, you will have to begin to gradually fade the food rewards after he has learned the skill.

Start out by skipping a food reward every other time your dog performs the skill. Instead of giving him the cue word *yes!* and food, you will give him a *good* and perhaps some petting as a reward. When he performs consistently at this level, you can begin to skip the food rewards more frequently. Eventually, you can stop offering food altogether for the particular command.

At this point, your dog's respect for you and his will to please you will inspire his obedience. If you have difficulty getting him to obey without food, make sure you are practicing good canine leadership skills, and focus on teaching as many power commands as possible.

## Negative Reinforcement
Two types of negative reinforcement can discourage unwanted behaviors.

## Formal Training Classes

This book is a fine tool for do-it-yourself trainers who want the flexibility to choose what, where, when, and how much to train their dogs. It is an excellent alternative to or supplement for training classes provided by professionals, but it does not replace them.

Formal training classes offer distinct advantages. They can provide motivation and structure for pet owners who find it difficult to stick to a regular schedule. The face-to-face interaction with a professional trainer can provide answers to questions, hands-on instruction, and personalized advice that cannot be acquired from a book. These classes may also offer the use of specialized training equipment, supplies, and facilities that may not be available at home. As if all this weren't enough, training classes provide opportunities to socialize your dog and to work with him in a distracting environment. If he learns to obey you amidst the clamor of other canines in the class, you will have a truly reliable pet.

If you do decide to enroll your dog in formal training classes, choose a reputable instructor. There are a number of things that reveal the quality of a trainer: attitude, education, and communication skills. If possible, sit in on one of the sessions before making a selection. Does the trainer maintain an upbeat attitude? Does she communicate effectively with both people and dogs? Is she accredited or certified by a national dog training organization? Does she use only positive training techniques? A basic obedience class can provide an excellent foundation for training any of the commands in this book.

Negative punishment involves *taking away* something your dog wants, such as withholding treats, withholding attention, or denying him the opportunity to do what he wants. Positive punishment involves *giving* your dog something he doesn't want, most often some form of physical punishment, which is never appropriate.

As much as we respect dogs' admirable traits—loyalty, devotion, and unconditional love, to name a few—they are, in some ways, very self-serving creatures. Dogs always behave in ways that bring them some reward or advantage. For example, a dog may pull on a leash to get his owner to walk faster, at a pace he wants. He may jump on people to release his pent-up energy, and hopefully (in his eyes), get some attention from his humans.

However, when the rewards of these behaviors are removed (a form of negative punishment), the behavior will become worthless to the dog, and he will eventually stop engaging in it. A dog who likes to pull on a leash to go faster will now go nowhere at all because his owner will stop walking. Such negative punishment is followed by the positive reinforcement of forward movement once the dog allows the leash to go slack again. A dog who likes to jump on people will receive no attention whatsoever until he keeps

> **Your dog needs plenty of repetition to perfect the new skills you teach him.**

his paws on the floor. Again, positive reinforcement in the form of attention and petting will be lavished on him when he behaves appropriately. This illustrates how negative punishment and positive reinforcement work together to shape behavior.

In a training situation, only negative punishments are appropriate because you do not want to dampen your dog's desire to learn. If you physically punish him (positive punishment), he may become frustrated, which will likely cause him to shut down and stop trying. Keep your dog's motivation high by simply withholding the reward of food or praise until he offers the correct behavior. It is never fair or productive to physically punish a dog, especially when he has not been taught what is expected of him.

Practice the commands your dog has learned in different locations and environments.

When addressing problem behaviors, you will achieve greater success by communicating clearly and consistently with your dog to let him know what you don't like and then redirecting him to a more appropriate behavior. Physical punishments will undermine his trust in you. While they may inspire your dog to comply out of fear, they will not nurture his will to please. So be a kind and patient teacher—the rewards will be enormous and the results will be long-lasting.

## Repetition

To get good at anything, you must practice. Your dog, too, needs plenty of repetition to perfect the skills you teach him. Repetition helps to condition him so that he will respond automatically to commands, and this conditioning contributes to reliable obedience. But repetition does not mean repeating a lesson until your dog goes crazy with boredom. You can tell when he has had enough if he begins to get distracted easily, ignores you, or yawns frequently. Communication is a two-way street, so always be observant of what your dog is trying to tell you with his body language and behavior.

To prevent boredom, vary the skills you work on during training sessions to keep things fresh and interesting. Introduce something new occasionally to challenge your dog. When you keep him engaged and mentally active, you'll be amazed at how much and how fast he can learn. Do not underestimate his intelligence.

Once your dog has become proficient in a particular skill, his training isn't over. You will need to provide a refresher lesson once in a while to keep it in good form. He may become rusty in skills that he rarely uses, so put him through all his paces from time to time. A good way to do this is to establish a practice routine that includes all the commands you've taught him so that you can go through them in order without forgetting or neglecting any of them.

## Consistency

Consistency is the yeast that turns dough into bread. It's the water that turns dust into concrete. And it's the magic potion that turns fractious canines into wonderful companions. Without it, all your training efforts are for naught. It's important to use training techniques, commands, and communication consistently. And you must have reliable expectations for your dog's behavior.

It might seem like a simple concept—to do things the same way all the time—but consistency is the one training component that tends to cause the greatest challenge for most dog owners. Why? It's not easy to establish new habits and stick to them. On the positive side, once a good habit is established, it is difficult to break. So make a conscious effort to handle your dog consistently, and before you know it, good canine manners will become as natural as sleeping and eating.

## Proofing

When you first teach your dog a new command, it's best to conduct your training in a quiet place where he can concentrate. Once he understands the meaning of a command, however, you'll need to teach him to respond to it in more distracting environments—a process called "proofing."

Practice your dog's new skills in different locations and environments: out in the yard, while on walks, or when visiting the pet store or veterinarian. Test him in the presence of distractions, like other dogs or animals, traffic noise, or crowds. Proofing helps to further condition him so that he will respond reliably. When you incorporate all

five elements of positive training—positive and negative reinforcements, repetition, consistency, and proofing—you will have a truly obedient pet.

Although all the elements of training help your dog develop trust in you, proofing helps you develop trust in your dog. There is no other way to determine if he will listen to you than to present him with a challenge that will test his self-control. With each test, his self-control will strengthen, and you will gain greater confidence in his obedience.

## TRAINING SUPPLIES

Any job, no matter how large or small, is always easier if you have the right equipment. This applies to dog training as well. There are a variety of tools, training aids, and props that can assist you in this process. Although some commands require no aids at all, others would be virtually impossible to teach without the assistance of specific equipment. Regardless of the type of training you desire to do, three basic necessities are a must: a collar, leash, and treats.

> Regardless of the type of training you desire to do, three basic necessities are a must: a collar, leash, and treats.

### Collar

For the purposes of this book, a properly fitted buckle collar is essential. It can be made of leather or nylon, and it should be of good quality so that the buckle will not come undone and the collar will not stretch out from use. Depending on the size of your dog, you should be able to fit one finger (for small dogs) or two fingers (for larger dogs) between the collar and your dog's neck, and he should not be able to slip out of it.

## Leash

The standard length for a training leash is 5 to 6 feet (1.5 to 2 m). It can be made of either leather or nylon, but purchase one appropriate for the size of your dog (1/2-inch [1.25-cm] wide for a small dog or 1-inch [2.5-cm] wide for a larger dog). It should have a secure snap on the end so that it can be attached to a collar.

## Treats

Remember that training treats should be small, about the size of the tip of your finger. Treats need to be appealing to your dog to motivate him, but that doesn't mean they can't be healthy. There are plenty of prepackaged ones on the market that are made of natural ingredients and contain no artificial preservatives. If you are inclined to make your own, you can find lots of recipes available online. You can even chop up some of your healthy leftovers, like grilled chicken, steak, or pot roast to use as food rewards. In general, dogs tend to prefer soft, moist treats. Avoid foods that are known to cause digestive upset, like dairy products.

Your dog, however, will be the ultimate judge. If he does not have sufficient interest in the treats you offer, they will be ineffective for training purposes. On the other hand, if they are too desirable, he may become overly excited and unable to concentrate on his lessons. Try several kinds and observe his reaction to them. You may very well decide to use different treats for different purposes. If your dog requires more motivation to master a difficult task, you can always resort to a more "high-powered" treat.

## Additional Supplies

In addition to the three basic necessities, there may be other supplies required for the various training exercises. You may wish to purchase and use a clicker instead of using the cue word *yes!* to mark behavior. Another very useful training aid is a long leash or rope, which will help you to work your dog from a distance and can assist you in training commands like *come*, which is the most important cue to teach your dog. Some tricks may require props, and some solutions for problem behaviors may require household items or specialty products. The training supplies necessary for each command are specified in the instructions.

Most of the items required for teaching the commands in this book are readily available at home or at a pet supply store. Always make sure to have your supplies assembled and ready to go before starting a training session. It is a time waster and concentration breaker to interrupt training to fetch items that are not on hand. If you are teaching tricks that require a number of props, make a list of the items needed ahead of time. As your dog's instructor, you need to come to class prepared!

**4**

# COMMUNICATING WITH YOUR DOG

**D**og training is all about communicating with your dog. The problem is that you won't be able to teach him anything if you can't understand each other. But think about how you would teach a foreigner to understand the English language if you didn't understand her native tongue. At first, you would probably communicate by pointing to objects, acting things out, or using hand signals, gestures, and facial expressions to represent your words until she became more fluent. You'll have to use a lot of these same techniques for teaching human language to your dog.

## BASIC VERBAL COMMUNICATION

Communication, in its simplest form, requires you to let your dog know what you like and what you don't like so that you can influence his behavior. Within the context of training, you also need to be able to let him know when you are releasing him from your control. Learning four basic communication words or cues—*yes!*, *good*, *okay*, and *uh-uh*—will allow you to teach your dog virtually anything you want.

### Pleasure Cues

*Yes!* is just one of two pleasure cues you will need to use to let your dog know when he is performing the correct behavior. *Good* is the other. The difference between them is that one is followed by a food reward and the other is

Learning four basic commands—*yes!*, *good*, *okay*, and *uh-uh*—will allow you to teach your dog virtually anything you want. The *good* command paired with petting lets him know when his behavior makes you happy.

not. Practice using both of these words in the appropriate situations in order to get the most value out of them.

## Yes!

### Description
This word lets the dog know when he's performed the correct behavior; it replaces the "click" in clicker training.

### Uses
Use *yes!* to bridge the time gap between your dog's behavior and the delivery of a food reward. It will also help sensitize him to your voice because he will begin to listen closely for this reward-based word.

### Prerequisites
None.

### Training Technique
This word can make it much easier to communicate with and train your dog. However, it does take a concerted effort to get in the habit of using it. When you first begin training your dog, focus on training yourself as well. With consistent use, this word can become amazingly powerful.

1. When training your dog with food rewards, say *yes!* whenever he performs the correct behavior. Then immediately give him a food reward. He will soon learn to associate the cue word *yes!* with food rewards and will work enthusiastically to earn more of them.
2. There are two important things to remember about the cue word *yes!*: It is always issued in a happy, upbeat voice, and it is always followed by a

food reward. Issuing this word in an excited tone helps to motivate your dog (this is why it includes an exclamation point), and consistently following it up with a food reward is what gives it value to him.

You also need a pleasure cue you can use when you do not intend to deliver a food reward. Once your dog has learned a particular command, you will want to encourage him to obey it without the

## Buddy Language

Communication is a magical thing. The rapport you develop with your dog makes it possible for you to understand each other like soul mates. If you make a habit of communicating frequently and consistently with him, and you pay close attention to his vocal and body signals as well, you might find that things as subtle as an eye movement can become meaningful pieces of communication. Others will be amazed by how your dog anticipates commands before you even say them, or how he executes impressive canine freestyle maneuvers without a visible cue from you. Eventually, you may even think you and your dog can read each other's minds. Perhaps this is because when you spend quality time together and communicate frequently, you begin to think alike.

incentive of receiving food. In addition, you can't always give him food every time he does something right (unless you happen to carry a bag of treats in your pocket at all times). In these cases, use the cue word *good* to let your dog know when his behavior makes you happy.

## Good

### Definition
This word lets the dog know his handler is pleased with his behavior.

### Uses
*Good* is a power command that offers praise and helps nurture the will to please, so don't be too stingy with it! Observe your dog, and try to catch him behaving correctly so that you can use the cue word *good*. This will allow you to keep your interactions with him as positive as possible. It's always preferable to tell your dog what he's doing right rather than what he's doing wrong.

### Prerequisites
None.

The communication signal *okay* lets your dog know you have released him from whatever command he is currently obeying.

## Training Technique

In the interest of simplicity and clarity, the cue word *good* is preferred over the alternative words *good boy* or *good girl*, as is not pairing this word with various other commands, such as *good sit* or *good down*, which some trainers tend to do. Helping your dog to understand the meaning of *good* depends more on consistent and frequent usage rather than actively training him. You must get in the habit of saying the cue word *good* whenever he engages in appropriate behaviors or activities. The use of this word is not limited to those times when your dog specifically obeys a command. You must be exceptionally observant and always let him know when he is acting in acceptable ways.

Some examples when *good* is appropriate to use include times when your dog greets other dogs calmly, when he stays close to you off leash, when he lies down nicely while you are eating dinner, or when he allows you to inspect his feet, ears, and other body parts.

Unlike the word *yes!*, which is spoken in an excited manner to motivate your dog during training, you should always issue *good* in a calm, subdued voice. In many situations, such as when greeting people or other dogs, you do not want to excite him; you want him to remain calm. Excitement can often spur a dog into undesirable behaviors, while calmness will help him maintain self-control.

Other suggestions for the use of this word include the following:

1. Use *good* in lieu of *yes!* when your dog obeys a command for which you do not intend to offer a food reward. This is an excellent transition word to use when weaning him off food rewards during the training process. You may pair this word with gentle petting to give it more value, provided that petting does not overstimulate him.

2. Use *good* whenever your dog remains calm in situations that normally excite him. This helps him master self-control over his natural instincts and makes him more responsive and obedient.

## Release Cue

Another basic communication word you should use frequently is *okay*. It releases your dog from a command and essentially grants him the freedom to be a dog. Expecting him to exercise the utmost discipline all the time can lead to frustration and unhappiness. However, if he can expect frequent releases to do his own thing, he'll be more willing to do whatever you ask of him.

## Okay (Also: Fine)

### Description

This is a training communication signal that lets your dog know you have released him from whatever command he is currently obeying.

### Uses

This word is a necessary part of basic communication, and you can use it in connection with many of the commands you teach your dog. It is especially useful with commands that have a duration component like *stay*. All dogs should become familiar with it, as it helps them understand their owner's expectations. For example, use it to let your dog know when he can eat the biscuit in the *balance the biscuit* trick or to release him from the *heel, stay, wait, leash on,* or *back off* commands.

## Prerequisites
None.

## Training Technique
This word does not have any specific prerequisites, but it does need to be used in conjunction with another command.

1. A simple wave of your hand when you say *okay* may be sufficient to let your dog know he is released from a command. You can also reinforce the meaning of this word when making him perform the *stay* and placing a treat on the floor some distance in front of him. You can use *okay* to release him to get the treat.
2. When teaching commands like *stay* and *wait*, remember to start out with very short durations so that your dog can learn to wait for the *okay* signal before he breaks the command. Once he gets in the habit of waiting for you to release him, you will be able to communicate to him exactly how long you'd like him to exercise the command.

## Displeasure Cue
Finally, you need a displeasure cue to let your dog know when he's doing something you don't like. The cue word *uh-uh* can serve this purpose. In any case where two different species befriend each other, the relationship works because each one expresses and interprets the other's pleasure and displeasure cues, and most importantly, they respect each other's cues. Your dog, too, must understand how you feel about his behavior and learn to respect the boundaries you communicate to him.

## Uh-Uh (Also: No, Shht)

### Description
The primary use of *uh-uh* is to address problem behaviors, such as jumping up, chewing, and barking. When you say this word, the dog should stop whatever he is doing

> A displeasure cue—*uh-uh*, *no*, or *shht*—lets your dog know when he's doing something you don't like.

and look to you for guidance. When you have his attention, redirect him to a more appropriate activity.

## Uses

This word lets your dog know when he is doing the wrong thing, going in the wrong direction, breaching his boundaries, or doing something you don't like. It can also be used to get him to stop in his tracks, a helpful safety feature if he is about to put himself in harm's way.

## Prerequisites
None.

## Training Technique

To communicate with your dog, you have to be able to quickly let him know when you are displeased with his behavior. But since *uh-uh* is obviously a negative word, there are some important rules concerning its use.

The consistent use of voice tones is just as important as the consistent use of commands when communicating vocally with your dog.

1. Never use *uh-uh* during a training session, as it will discourage your dog from attempting to learn. How would you like to get your hand slapped every time you got a math problem wrong? Pretty soon, you would stop attempting to answer math problems. For the same reason, it is best to ignore incorrect responses from your dog during training sessions and focus

on telling him what to do rather than what not to do. It is very important to keep training experiences as positive as possible.

2. When you use *uh-uh* to let your dog know he is doing something you don't like, such as chewing on your shoes or jumping on you, issue it sharply and firmly to interrupt the inappropriate behavior. Then, always be prepared to redirect your dog to an appropriate behavior or activity for which you can praise him. This way, your interactions always conclude on a positive note.

3. Your dog will learn this word quickly if you use it consistently to interrupt inappropriate behavior. But you do not necessarily have to wait until he is already engaged in an inappropriate behavior to use it. You can also use it as a warning if you know your dog is about to do something you don't like. Once he understands what *uh-uh* means, he should immediately stop what he's doing whenever he hears it.

## CONSISTENT VOICE TONES

The consistent use of voice tones is just as important as the consistent use of commands when communicating vocally with your dog. He pays attention to both. Just as the basic communication words *yes!*, *good*, *okay*, and *uh-uh* should each have their own consistent tones, any other commands you teach should also have specific tones. The cue *who's here?* will not generate the same response from your dog if it does not possess the final uplift in tone that makes it a question. *Hey!* may not get his attention if you do not say it sharply. If you issue a command in different voice tones, it will not have as clear a meaning to him as it would if you issued it in a consistent tone.

Consistency is the main ingredient for canine language comprehension. Not only do you need to use consistent tones for the commands you teach your dog, you also have to be careful to use the words themselves consistently. Remember that "come by me," "get your butt over here," and "you better come here this instant" are not the same as using the cue word *come*. It's very easy to talk to dogs as if they are human, but they're not. They don't have the same language capabilities as humans. They may be intelligent enough to figure out what their owners mean when they say, "you better get off that couch," simply by interpreting voice tone. But wouldn't you rather have a dog who *really* understands the words you're saying? If so, teach him *off*, and use it each and every time you want him to get off the couch.

## HAND AND BODY SIGNALS

Dogs may not have the same verbal skills as humans, but their mastery of body language more than makes up for it. They are so adept at picking up subtle body cues that you may even wonder if your dog is psychic. Humans, on the other hand, have become so dependent on spoken language that they often neglect to pay attention to body signals. To communicate clearly with your dog, you'll need to get in the habit of not only observing his body signals but also being

conscious of your own. No matter how cheerfully you say the cue word *come*, your dog isn't likely to obey if you appear to be angry.

Because most body signals are given unconsciously, it's best to control your emotions and maintain a happy, relaxed attitude when working with your dog. If you find yourself becoming frustrated, you can bet your dog will sense it. Negative body signals will put him in a negative and stressful state of mind as well. When this occurs, your training efforts will result in little progress. He will be reluctant to do what you want, or he may refuse to do anything at all. When you find yourself having difficulty maintaining a cheerful demeanor during a training session, end it until you can regain a more positive outlook. Always remember that you can't hide your feelings from your dog!

Dogs learn body language signals faster than verbal cues.

Your dog's expertise in body language does provide some important advantages. Namely, it makes him exceptionally sensitive to hand signals. Many of the training techniques in this book provide instructions on how to progress to hand signals for various skills. They are useful for reinforcing the meaning of a command or communicating with your dog when loud noise or distance makes verbal communication difficult.

If you choose to teach your dog a hand signal, consider teaching him to respond to the verbal command as well. There may be times when your hands are in use and you cannot communicate with them. Alternatively, there may be times when it is difficult to issue a verbal command, and a hand signal will work better. Condition your dog to respond to either type of communication by issuing them separately, rather than at the same time, during training. For instance, say the command first and then give the hand signal.

## CANINE COMMUNICATION

Communication works two ways: If you want to teach your dog how to understand your language, you need to be able to understand his as well. Most conflicts between humans and canines occur because dogs don't understand humans or humans don't understand dogs.

Although this book is primarily devoted to teaching your dog human language in the form of commands, it is just as important for you to learn how to interpret canine language. Of course, this isn't just a matter of interpreting various vocal cues and body signals; it's also about understanding the culture and context of your dog's behavior and current environment. Study his vocal and physical expressions, and then put them in the context of his frame of mind to get the full meaning of what he is trying to tell you.

When you are interpreting what your dog is "saying," you also need to consider that dogs are individuals, and as such,

**Hand signals are useful for reinforcing the meaning of a command.**

they each speak a little differently. Just like people, some are more communicative than others and they each favor different gestures. A high-strung dog may yawn frequently to relieve tension, while another dog may only yawn when he feels stressed. Some dogs bare their front teeth in a submissive "smile," while others never smile at all. It is up to you to learn your dog's way of speaking, or his individual dialect, so to speak. Observe him as much as possible to become familiar with his way of expressing himself.

## Body Language

Like other animals, dogs are honest communicators. The only time they "lie" is when they need to bluff to prevent conflicts and preserve the social hierarchy. For the most part, however, they wear their hearts on their sleeves (or bodies) in the form of body language. This is largely an expression of their current mental state, which is communicated subconsciously. For example, dogs don't consciously raise or lower their tails to convey submission or dominance; their bodies simply reflect the way they feel.

Being able to recognize these gestures is only a part of the story; you need to get in the habit of noticing

**Dogs communicate with each other using a vast array of body language.**

communication signals. Since humans do not naturally pay attention to such things, try to make a conscious effort to read canine body language every time you see a dog. Besides evaluating your own dog's postures and facial expressions, observe other dogs you see in the neighborhood or at the vet's office. You'll be amazed to learn just how much they really have to say, and you'll become an expert at interpreting these signals as you gain practice.

## Canine Body Expressions

Canine body expressions are spoken with the entire body, which means that the position of the body, tail, head, ears, mouth, and eyes must all be taken into consideration to determine the correct interpretation. Canines do not always express their emotions in black-and-white terms—they may display different combinations of body signals if they feel conflicted about a situation, and they may also have their own unique ways of expressing themselves.

## Vocal Language

Anyone who is not used to communicating with dogs may think that a bark is a bark is a bark, but this couldn't

| Expression | Body | Head | Eyes | Ears | Mouth | Tail |
|---|---|---|---|---|---|---|
| dominant | tall and erect | high | forward | forward | closed, relaxed | high, wagging |
| dominant-aggressive | tall and tense, piloerection | high | direct stare | forward, stiff | tight-lipped or teeth-baring | high, stiff |
| guarded | tall and tense, piloerection | high | sideways glance | forward and/or back | tight-lipped | high, stiff |
| nervous or scared | crouched | level or low | sideways glance | back or alternating between forward and back | tight-lipped | low and stiff or between legs |
| fear-aggressive | crouched and tense | level or low | sideways glance | back | tight-lipped or teeth-baring | low or between legs |
| relaxed | tall and relaxed | level | soft | low or splayed | open, relaxed | level |
| submissive | crouched | low | averted | low or back | closed, lip-licking | low |
| friendly | level | level or low | soft | low or back | "smile," open, relaxed | level or low, wagging |
| excited | animated | high | bright | forward | open | level, wagging profusely |
| playful | play bow | level or high | bright | forward | open | level, wagging |
| stressed | level or crouched | level or low | averted | back | open, tense, yawning | level or low |

be further from the truth. Canines have a very rich vocal repertoire. There are yips and whines and grunts and howls, and all of them have a different meaning, depending on their context.

The best way to learn your dog's vocal language is to pay attention to it. When you listen to him and observe him closely, you will quickly learn the difference between the bark that means "I *think* I heard something" and the bark that means "I *definitely* heard something." You'll be able to distinguish between yips of excitement and yips of pain. You'll know whether your dog is growling in play or growling in warning.

It's easy to ignore a dog's vocal expressions, especially in the case of an excessively "talkative" individual, but your dog is more likely to communicate in meaningful ways when he knows you take him seriously. When he barks at something, take the time to investigate what has grabbed his attention. Respond to his vocal communications and teach him the *quiet* command (see Chapter 9) so that you can let him know when he is using his voice inappropriately.

## Behavioral Language

Behavioral language is a form of language that's often overlooked. Behavior can reveal a lot about a human or animal's thoughts and feelings. Yet when it appears to be negative, it is too often dismissed as "naughtiness," "a bad mood," or "a lack of self-control." Try to look at your dog's behavior, whether it is good or bad, from a deeper perspective. What is he trying to say with it?

It's obvious that if your dog brings his toys to you, he's trying to convince you to play

## Communicating Through Handling

Teaching your dog what to do and how to do it occasionally requires some hands-on interaction, but there is a difference between physical manipulation and physical force. Never try to force your dog into a position. Pushing on his rump, back, or neck, or pulling on his legs, can injure him, and this type of instruction is not very effective. Whenever possible, lure your dog into the proper position with encouragement, praise, or treats. For example, a treat held over his head will encourage him to beg, back up, or sit down. A treat held at floor level will encourage him to drop his head or lie down. Dogs learn faster when they discover how to move their bodies on their own rather than having their bodies "modeled" into position.

with him. If he sits by the door, he wants to go outside. If he rolls onto his back, he wants you to scratch his tummy. Be sure to apply the same type of behavioral interpretations to your dog's undesirable behaviors as well. If your dog tears apart the house while you are gone, he may be trying to tell you that he is lonely and stressed. If he piddles in the house, he may be trying to tell you that he needs to go outside more frequently or regularly. Figuring out what he is trying to tell you is the first step toward solving any problem behavior.

There is always a reason behind a dog's behavior. It's easy to conclude that he is just being "stupid" or "goofy," but it is much more productive to determine his true motivation. You may need to consider his individual personality traits to determine what he is expressing. You may also need to take into account his lifestyle, outside influences, or his environment to put it into proper context. But when you can decipher your dog's behavior, it will open your eyes to his world and facilitate a much more meaningful discourse between the two of you.

## SETTING YOUR DOG UP FOR SUCCESS

Your dog has a lot of untapped potential, but there is only one way he will realize it—you have to teach him. You can certainly jump right into the training techniques in this book and begin teaching commands, but there are a few things that can help improve your chances of success.

### Exercise First

Horse trainers have long recognized the benefits of exercising equines prior to training them. It's a good way of "getting the kinks out" so that the animal can settle down and focus on his lessons. Even schoolchildren enjoy better concentration in the classroom when they have recess breaks to let off some steam. So why not provide the same physical outlet for your dog prior to training?

Exercise prior to training is especially beneficial for high-energy breeds that have difficulty focusing, but it can help any dog to relax and concentrate better. A game of fetch, an opportunity to run in an enclosed area, or even a short, brisk walk can result in greater attention and faster learning. Training programs that offer playtime for the dogs at the end of their sessions would be better off providing it first rather than last!

If you exercise your dog prior to training, remember that the purpose of it is to help calm him down and build up his self-control; it is not to exhaust him. Be careful not to overdo a good thing. A tired dog is just as unfocused and distracted as one who is hyped up with too much energy. If you engage in a physically exerting form of activity, give your dog a chance to cool down and calm down before beginning your training session.

### Attention

Successful communication requires two elements: a sender and a receiver. When communication is sent but not received, it fails. This is why it is so important to pay attention to what your dog is trying to tell you with his vocal, body, and behavioral language. But it also underscores the importance of having your dog's attention when you send your own communication signals.

Regardless of the popularity of the buzzword "multitasking," human (and canine) brains are not really designed to focus on more than one thing at a time. Thus, when people text while driving, they get into accidents, and when your dog has his attention focused on something else, like another animal, he acts like he can't hear you. You must first establish contact with your dog before you can effectively communicate with

him, and the best way to do this is to teach him to be responsive to his name.

1. To improve your dog's name recognition, carry treats around with you and say his name occasionally. If he looks at you when you say it, give him a treat. Keep in mind that his name is an attention-getter, not a synonym for the *come* command. When you say it, he should look at you as if he is asking, "What?"

2. Sometimes, your dog may become so distracted that he won't respond to his name. In this case, you'll have to use other methods to get his attention. You can use the cue word *hey!*, gently nudge him with your hand, or make a noise. You need to be able to break his concentration so that he can focus on what you are saying to him. Your dog doesn't necessarily have to look at you to pay attention to you, but he does need to obey you when you give him a command.

Exercise prior to training is especially beneficial for high-energy breeds that have difficulty focusing.

## Keep It Short

Humans have a love affair with words, so much so that they often don't know when to stop talking. Although we usually speak in sentences with other humans, we need to break down our language into its smallest units if we want dogs to understand it. Single words are much easier for them to distinguish than strings of words, which are about as meaningful to them as saying, "Blah-blah-blah-blah."

For instance, saying, "Come," is preferable to "Come over here." When a dog can't discern individual words, he has to rely on voice tone to decipher what a person is saying.

Whenever you begin to attach extraneous words to simple commands, you convolute your communication signals and increase the chance of miscommunication. Although most dogs are smart enough to figure out what some word combinations mean, like "do you want a treat?" and "let's go for a car ride," confusion is sure to set in when you say, "I'll give you the treat in my pocket if you beg for me." Avoid potential miscommunications by getting in the habit of using simple commands and communication signals. When you use words consistently, your dog will understand what they mean in all situations without having to wonder if he heard the word "treat" in that long string of sounds.

Training sessions don't need to be long to be effective. Just 20 minutes a day will bring results.

The units of communication you use are not the only things you need to keep short. You should also limit the duration of your training sessions. Ten minutes is long enough for a puppy, and 20 minutes is usually sufficient for adult dogs. A dog is likely to lose focus and interest during sessions that last longer than 30 minutes. In this regard, most formal training classes are too long for dogs, but realize that their primary purpose is to teach training techniques to owners. The majority of training needs to be conducted at home during brief sessions.

# Communicating With a Clicker

There is an intermediate form of communication that dogs (and many other animal species) tend to understand quite readily. It's called "clicker training." Marine mammal trainers first used it with dolphins and killer whales more than 40 years ago. The fact that they used whistles instead of clickers does not change the pure and simple concepts behind this type of training. Clicker training involves giving the animal a sound cue and food rewards for performing desired behaviors, and such positive reinforcement, of course, encourages the animal to repeat the desired behaviors. Dogs, being highly food motivated, are perfect candidates for this type of training.

Food would be the perfect communication tool if it weren't for one crucial drawback: timing. In order for an animal to understand which behavior the trainer is rewarding, he must receive the food reward while engaged in the desired behavior. Unfortunately, this isn't always possible. There may be a distance that separates the trainer from the animal and makes it difficult to deliver a food reward fast enough for it to be effective. This is where the clicker comes in.

The clicker is a small, handheld noisemaking device that allows the trainer to "mark" the desired behavior. Each time the animal hears a click, the trainer subsequently rewards him with food. Animals quickly learn that the click means they will receive food, and they will attempt to get more by repeating the behaviors that earn clicks. Trainers often refer to the clicker as a "bridge" because it fills the gap between a desired behavior and the delivery of a food reward.

Some trainers like the distinctive noise of the clicker because dogs become very reactive to it, but it does have a few disadvantages. It can be a challenge to find a spare hand to hold a clicker while manipulating a dog and handling a leash. From a communications standpoint, it doesn't do much good to teach a dog to be sensitive to the sound of a clicker if your goal is to have him become responsive to your voice. Fortunately, you can solve both problems by using the cue word *yes!* as a marker in place of the click. When you consistently back up this cue word with a food reward, your dog will quickly associate it with food. It will become the "magic word" that he craves to hear, and he will begin to listen carefully for it during training sessions. *Yes!* is one of four mandatory basic communication words, or cues, that you must learn to use consistently and appropriately so that your dog can learn to understand you.

## Make It Clear

Every command you teach your dog should have its own sound, tone, and context. Words that sound too much alike may confuse him; hence, the command entries in this book provide alternative command words whenever possible so that you can choose words that are easy for your dog to distinguish. In cases where sound-alike words apply to completely different situations, such as *seek* and *speak*, miscommunication isn't as likely to occur.

Clarity is just as important in hand signals and body language as it is in spoken language. When using food rewards as lures in training and then fading these motions into hand signals, it's easy to end up with many that look similar. Think about what kind of unique hand signal you eventually want to fade into before you start training a new skill. This will help you avoid inadvertently duplicating one you've already taught your dog. For instance, if you've already taught him that a circular motion with your finger indicates *spin*, be careful not to use the same motion to indicate *roll over*. Devise a new hand signal to signify it, such as flipping your hand from palm up to palm down.

When owners don't speak in ways that are easy to understand, dogs tend to get in the habit of ignoring human communication signals. But when you speak clearly to your dog and use words in the proper tone and context, he will become much more responsive to you.

> Every dog is born with his own individual mix of talent and potential and will learn at his own pace.

Isn't that the kind of relationship you've always wanted to have with your canine companion?

## Consistency

As I've already stated several times: If you want your dog to understand you, you must use language consistently. You might get tired of hearing this, but it is the single most important component of effective human–canine communication. It is also the one element that seems to cause the greatest challenge for most people.

It's hard to abandon communication habits that began in toddlerhood, when strings of words first began to roll off our tongues. We all grew up learning how to communicate with other humans, but speaking with dogs requires slightly different language rules. While it's common practice to put a period at the end of every sentence when talking with humans, we have to learn to put a period at the end of every word when we talk to dogs.

Learning how to use our native language differently is almost as difficult as learning a foreign language. No wonder so many owners persist in talking to their dogs as if they were humans! Sometimes it seems easier to allow barriers to exist rather than to change the way we do things. But if you are up for the challenge and make the commitment to establish better lines of communication with your dog, the benefits are enormous.

Consistently talking to him in ways he can really understand will produce more than a dog who listens better—it will take your relationship to a whole new level. It will open

doors for you and provide opportunities for you to do things and go places together that you wouldn't otherwise be able to do. Do you have your heart set on doing therapy dog work? Do you want to travel with your dog without worrying about his manners? Do you want to participate in canine sports or enjoy trips to the dog park without concern about his behavior? Problem behaviors will become a thing of the past, and you'll be able to enjoy the best that dog ownership has to offer. Most importantly, the consistent communication habits you develop will last you a lifetime, and you'll be able to apply them to your interactions with any dog.

## Keep Training Sessions Positive

Dog training isn't without its challenges, and things may not always go smoothly. Since your dog's attitude is a reflection of your own, it pays to keep things positive and learn to recognize when negativity is seeping in. Try to keep your sense of humor and have reasonable expectations. You'll also find that you have a lot more patience if you do not put a time limit on your dog's learning. Every dog has his own strengths and weaknesses and will learn in his own way.

Training should be something you both enjoy. It should help you develop a closer relationship rather than drive a wedge between you. Whether your session is pleasurable or trying, it's important to end it with a smile. Before you put the treats away, ask your dog to do a trick or skill he knows well so that you can reward him and you can both continue to look forward to working together again.

# 5

# BASIC TRAINING

A well-rounded training curriculum will nurture your dog's social development and provide life skill instruction as well. He needs to learn a few basics so that he can develop healthy relationships and adapt to life in a human household. Socialization, crate training, and housetraining are not only necessary to make it easy to live with him, they also have a profound effect on his future, for dogs who are deficient in these skills often find themselves with a one-way ticket to the animal shelter.

Believe it or not, your dog may have already received some instruction before you even acquired him. As a puppy, he may have learned that his siblings would not want to play with him if he was too rough. If he was kept in a clean environment, he may have learned to prefer cleanliness, and so a part of his housetraining has already been addressed. However, it may also be possible that your dog had no preliminary instruction at all, or worse, he may have been mistaught. Perhaps he was orphaned and had no early experiences in socialization with his siblings and mother. Perhaps he was kept in a dirty environment and learned that living in those conditions was normal and acceptable.

Regardless of your dog's earlier education, it's up to you to give him every opportunity to excel in these basics. And the best time to start this type of training is

**As soon as a puppy is born, he begins to learn communication skills and boundaries from his mother and siblings.**

immediately after you bring him home so that good habits can be established from the very beginning.

## SOCIALIZATION

The importance of socialization in dog training is finally receiving the emphasis it deserves. This developmental process shapes your dog's perceptions of the world and thus influences his behavior in profound ways. When a puppy is born, he doesn't have any social skills. He doesn't know what he should be afraid of or what he should feel safe around. He doesn't know how to communicate, other than demonstrating the primal reactions to hunger and pain with which nature endowed him. He must learn everything through experience and training.

The minute a puppy is born, he learns certain communication skills and boundaries from his mother and siblings, which is why it is important not to remove a puppy from his mother until he is at least eight weeks old. He also goes through a fear imprint stage between 6 and 12 weeks of age. If he suffers a frightening incident associated with people, animals, objects, or places during this time, he may develop a deep-rooted fear of those things. This is a critical age to provide pleasant experiences.

But what if your dog is already an adult? You can't change his past experiences, but you can still provide opportunities for him to develop healthy perceptions of the world around him. How you go about socializing him may depend somewhat on his personality. If he is a protective breed, you may want to focus extra attention on his socialization to people so that he will not grow to think all strangers are untrustworthy. If he tends to get nervous in new situations, you may want to put extra work into confidence-building activities, like training classes, dog sports, or getting him out and about as much as possible. If he is reactive to other dogs, you may want to participate in a special training class that will help desensitize him to the presence of other dogs.

### People

Socialization helps your dog accept and befriend your guests, family members, and friendly strangers you may encounter

## Old Dog, New Friends

There is no age limit for reaping the benefits of socialization. Even older dogs adopted from shelters can learn new social skills. There are an abundance of stories about abused or neglected dogs whose personalities transformed incredibly after being properly and carefully socialized. Socialization allows a dog to reach his true potential. It helps alleviate fears and builds confidence. It nurtures patience and tolerance. It teaches him how to cope with stress and change. So don't deny your dog opportunities for socialization, regardless of his age.

during normal daily activities. It's important to give him as many positive experiences with people as possible.

1. Take your dog on frequent walks, and stop to chat with your neighbors once in a while. Bring him with you to the pet store, park, or any other place where dogs are allowed. If you want to participate in organized walks or dog sports, you can socialize him to both people and dogs at the same time!

2. Make a point of exposing your dog to many different types of people. This includes men, women, tall people, short people, people who wear hats, and even people who use canes or wheelchairs. And don't forget that children are people, too! If you don't have any of your own, you may want to invite some neighborhood kids over to have a playdate with your dog.

3. During socialization exercises, always make sure the experience is a positive one for your dog. Also, always supervise all interactions to keep him and anyone he meets safe. With proper training, he will learn to trust people and perceive them as generally friendly and trustworthy.

4. A useful command to teach your dog is *say hi*, which is covered in Chapter 10. This is an excellent cue word that tells your dog you have evaluated the situation and determined that a person or animal is safe to approach. Consider teaching commands that encourage him to respect people's personal space, like *move* and *off* from Chapter 9, and *back off* from Chapter 10. They can help round out your dog's social education.

## Animals and Pets

Do you have other pets in your household? Do you want to participate in activities involving other dogs? Do you want to be able to walk your dog without having him bark every time another animal crosses your path? These are all good reasons to socialize your dog to other animals.

When it comes to introducing your dog to other household pets, it's important to take things slow and easy. First impressions are extraordinarily important to animals, so you want to be sure all your pets have positive experiences with each other from the very beginning.

1. When introducing your dog to cats or other species, begin by letting them get accustomed to each other's scent. Keep them separated by doors or gates until they begin to show signs of feeling comfortable in each other's presence. This will become obvious when their curiosity and excitement wanes, and they begin to ignore each other occasionally. Allow them to meet each other when they appear calm and relaxed, with your dog on a leash in case you must separate them. Many dogs develop interspecies relationships that are quite close.

2. If you need to introduce your dog to another resident canine, this is best accomplished with the assistance of another person so that you can have both dogs on leashes. When allowing them to meet each other, keep the leashes slack, as tight leashes can make dogs feel restricted and vulnerable. Allow the two to sniff each

other briefly, and then say, "Okay, that's enough," and pull them apart. Brief greetings will minimize the chance of either dog feeling threatened or becoming aggressive.

3. One of the best ways for dogs to become accustomed to each other is to take them for a walk together, again with the assistance of another person to keep them under separate control. Dogs who travel together often form a very close bond. Sometimes it's immediately obvious that two dogs will become the best of friends. At other times, it may take a little time for them to feel comfortable with each other. Remember, dogs are individuals, too, and some personalities go together better than others. Fortunately, they are naturally very social creatures, and with time and patience most learn to cohabitate quite well together.

4. There are a number of commands in this guide that can help your dog learn how to respond appropriately to other animals. *Say hi* is a good general greeting command that can be used when meeting either people or dogs. Other useful commands include *quiet* (if your dog tends to bark at other animals) and *leave it* (when your dog is overly focused on another dog or animal) from Chapter 9, and *walk on* (to get your dog to pass by another dog) from Chapter 10.

Just as dogs need socialization with a variety of people, they also need socialization with a variety of other animals.

## New Situations

How will your dog react when you have to move to another home? How will he adjust to the new baby in the household? How will he handle being left in a kennel when you go on vacation? Adaptability is a very important quality. Your dog's tolerance for change may depend somewhat on his personality, but you can, to some extent, help him develop the coping skills he'll need to handle new situations well.

1. Try to change things up occasionally. As much as you and your dog love to go for a walk every day, skip a day at least once a week so that he can learn to adapt to a change in routine. When you go for walks, change your route occasionally.

2. Although keeping your dog on a regular feeding schedule helps regulate his system, don't feel guilty if you must delay his dinner for an hour due to unforeseen circumstances—consider it valuable training in coping skills.

3. If you've ever been to a dog show, you may have been amazed by how calm and comfortable some of the show dogs appeared to be in the midst of all the excitement and activity. Many owners begin taking their puppy prodigies to shows at a young age to accustom them to that type of environment. Take your dog to a variety of places, too, so that he can learn to adapt to unfamiliar environments with a minimum of anxiety.

The time and effort you put into socializing your dog is never wasted. With each new, positive experience, he becomes more confident and well adjusted.

## Dog Park Confidential

Dog parks are growing immensely in popularity, and if you don't already have one in your community, you may soon. They provide excellent opportunities for exercise and socialization with both humans and other dogs. They also provide the same benefits for people! However, be aware that these parks are not for every dog. If you are interested in taking your dog to one, make sure he:

- already gets along with other dogs (the dog park is not the place to teach him this)
- already gets along with people
- is large enough to fend for himself (unless there is a separate area for small dogs)
- has had all of his puppy vaccinations or is up to date on adult vaccinations
- has learned and responds to basic obedience commands

Commands you might find useful at a dog park include *say hi* (for greeting people or dogs), *this way* (to tell your dog which direction to go), and *wait up* (so your dog will wait for you), all from Chapter 10. Also, consider teaching your dog *leave it* from Chapter 9. Dog parks are often fenced and can be a safe place to train many off-leash skills, so don't forget to bring treats.

## CRATE TRAINING

Crate training tends to receive a bad rap because of misconceptions about what it entails. After all, isn't it cruel to keep a dog in a cage? Surprisingly, the answer is both yes and no. Yes, crating a dog can be cruel if the crate is misused or abused. However, if used judiciously, crating is a perfectly safe and humane method of confinement. If you have doubts, attend any dog show—you will see many dogs comfortably reclining in their crates without fussing. These animals have learned that the crate is a place of comfort and refuge, not a prison.

Imagine the benefits of having a dog who willingly enters his crate and will stay there for periods of time without barking, whining, or clamoring to get out. You could confine him when repairmen need to come and go from your home. You could separate him from the children when their interactions become overly rambunctious. You could easily confine your dog when you are unable to supervise him during parties, while moving, or when you need to keep him from getting under foot. And you would be able to travel easily with him because a crate is a safe place to keep him while in transit.

So how do you convince your dog that the crate is a desirable place for him

> A crate is a valuable tool for housetraining and keeping your dog safe when you cannot supervise him.

to spend time? Fortunately, his canine instincts can help you. Thousands of years of domestication haven't erased millions of years of canine evolution, and one of the instincts dogs inherited from their ancestors is the very foundation of crate training. Nature has programmed them to appreciate the comfort of small, confined, den-like places, and crate training basically awakens the instinct to seek such shelter in a crate.

There are some important rules concerning their proper use, which will help contribute to your success and your dog's happiness.

1. If you want your dog to develop a positive perception of his crate, you must make it as comfortable as possible and enable him to establish it as his own personal domain. This means you should not allow children or other animals to play in it. Keep a bed and perhaps a few toys in it. Feeding your dog inside his crate is another good way to help him feel more content in it.

2. Never use the crate in a punitive manner because, again, your dog's willingness to use it depends on his positive perceptions of it. Never crate him for excessively long periods of time. If you need to confine your dog for periods longer than six hours, use door gates or a puppy pen to provide him with a larger confinement area.

3. Use an appropriately sized crate. Your dog should be able to lie down,

## No Crate? No Problem!

Crate training is not always practical or necessary. If you have a very large dog, a crate may take up more room than you can spare. Maybe your dog, due to his particular personality or past experiences, has exceptional difficulty adjusting to confinement. Or perhaps you do not feel comfortable using a crate or prefer to allow your dog to sleep on your bed. In lieu of a crate, it is always a good idea to provide a "safe zone" to which he can retreat from high-stress situations. This should be a quiet area off limits to children or other animals. (A door gate or pet door can help provide a necessary barrier.) Always provide your dog with a comfortable pet bed, blanket, or rug on which to rest. Instead of teaching him the *kennel* command, teach him the *place* command in Chapter 9 so that you can tell him when and where to go lie down.

If you choose to allow your dog on your bed, always make it clear to him that it is your bed and not his. He should understand that being allowed to sleep there is a privilege, and if he ever abuses that privilege by becoming possessive of it or refusing to move when he has made you uncomfortable, do not feel guilty or hesitate to use the *off* command (covered in Chapter 9) to revoke this privilege.

stand up, and turn around comfortably in it. When using the crate as a housetraining aid, it is important not to use one that is too large because your dog may use a portion of it to do his business. Rather than buying larger crates as your puppy grows, a more economical option is to purchase one with a divider that allows you to adjust the size of the space.

4. Always give your dog a potty break prior to confinement. Set him up to succeed.

5. The *kennel* command in Chapter 9 provides the specific steps necessary for proper crate training. This is a process that takes some time to complete, so do not attempt to rush through it. Your patience will pay off by having a dog who is willing and cooperative when it's time to go to bed or be confined.

## HOUSETRAINING

The fact that dogs are trainable has not only made them great companions for humans, but it has also allowed them to live in our homes with little restriction or confinement. Housetraining is necessary in helping them become welcome household members, and fortunately, dogs have a natural desire to keep their living space clean. But they generally apply this concept to a much smaller, den-like area. Housetraining, then, becomes a matter of teaching your dog to apply this concept to the larger space of your home.

This can be a challenging and frustrating process, especially if it involves frequent cleanups, but there are several

### Crate, Sweet Crate

As your dog's surrogate den, his crate should be his own personal space. It should be a place of refuge, where he can rest when he's tired and retreat to when he is stressed or overwhelmed. However, the crate cannot fulfill your dog's instinctual needs or contribute to his emotional well-being if the peace of his personal shelter is disturbed.

Do not allow children or other pets to play in or around your dog's place of respite. Keep his crate in a quiet location away from the hustle and bustle of your busy household, and enforce a "do not disturb" rule when he is in it. This will not only create greater comfort for him, but it may also contribute to his good behavior.

things you can do to avoid the frustration, minimize accidents, and ensure success.

1. Do not expect your dog to learn housetraining in a specific period of time. Dogs are individuals who learn at their own pace. Even different sizes and breeds of dogs have diverse learning curves when it comes to this concept. Puppies do not have much bladder control until they are several months old, and adopted adult dogs may experience a lapse in housetraining due to the stresses

of adjusting to a new home or new diet. Some dogs take up to a year to become reliably housetrained, so try to approach this training with realistic expectations.

2. Be vigilant in supervising your dog carefully indoors until he is housetrained. Always confine him to a crate or puppy pen when you can't watch him. If you want to avoid cleanups and prevent your dog from developing undesirable habits, you must avoid giving him the opportunity to mess in the house.

3. Never punish your dog for housetraining lapses. It is not fair or productive to punish him because he hasn't learned something yet. He will learn much faster if you keep the training process positive and rewarding.

Designate a potty area outdoors. The smells that become established there will encourage your dog to do his business whenever you take him to that spot.

The following steps will help you housetrain your dog in the most efficient manner.

1. Designate a potty area outdoors. The smells that become established there will encourage your dog to do his business whenever you take him to that spot.

2. Establish a confinement area. This is the place where you will keep your dog when you cannot supervise him. You may use a crate, puppy pen, or room with door gate barriers. A crate is a perfect place to confine your dog for short periods of time when you cannot supervise him because most dogs will try not to eliminate in their small den-like living quarters. Provide a potty break prior to confinement, and never confine your dog for periods longer than the recommended amount of time for his age. With time, patience, and proper management, your dog will begin to understand that your entire house is a waste-free zone.

   For larger confinement areas, make sure your dog's space is pet-safe—that is, there should be no electrical cords to chew on, garbage to get into, houseplants to eat, or other potential hazards. Larger confinement areas also require an appropriate area for elimination. You can put newspaper on the floor or use commercially available wee-wee pads. When cleaning up messes, it helps to save a little bit of the soiled paper to put down with the clean supply, as the scent will encourage your dog to use the paper. Wee-wee pads are already scented for this purpose.

3. Strictly control your dog's freedom in the home, and observe him carefully until he is reliably housetrained. If he begins walking in circles, sniffing the floor, arching his back, squatting, or lifting a leg, these are indications that he is about to eliminate. Interrupt the behavior with a sharp *uh-uh* and then give the *outside* command (you can find it in Chapter 9) as you whisk your dog to his designated outdoor potty area. Food rewards can help expedite the housetraining process, so be prepared to say "yes!" and reward him when he potties in the right place.

4. You can greatly improve your dog's chance of success if you keep him on a regular eating, sleeping, and potty break schedule. He will put more effort into "holding it" if he knows when to expect the next potty break. This schedule should include taking him to his potty area at times when he's most likely to need to go, such as right after eating, sleeping, or playing.

5. When your dog understands the cue word *outside*, you can begin to use it to ask him if he needs to eliminate. He may develop his own response to this word—he may get excited, run to the door, or jump up and down. If you want your dog to display a more specific response, consider teaching him *ring the bell* from Chapter 12. As with all other training, preventing household accidents is all about effective communication.

   Another command you may want to consider incorporating into your housetraining efforts is *go potty*, which is covered in Chapter 10.

# 6

# MANAGING PROBLEM BEHAVIORS

eaching your dog various commands can improve his vocabulary, strengthen the bond you share, and result in having a more responsive and obedient canine companion—but it can also help solve problem behaviors. The advantage of using specific commands to teach good canine manners is that it can turn a negative into a positive: Instead of telling your dog what not to do, commands allow you to tell him what to do.

## MEETING YOUR DOG'S NEEDS

As powerful as verbal communication can be in influencing your dog's behavior, it does have its limitations. It will have little effect if you have not first met his needs. For example, would you listen to someone who told you not to drink a glass of water if you just finished running a marathon and felt dehydrated? You also need to understand canine behavior to determine when prevention is necessary to support the commands you use. You cannot change a dog into a human, but you can take steps to make it easier for him to successfully live in a human world.

Dogs have a number of basic requirements, such as food, shelter, companionship, leadership, instinct

Many canine problem behaviors arise from physical or emotional needs that are unfulfilled.

fulfillment, and exercise. The strength of these needs depends entirely on your dog's individual personality (or breed). A majority of problem behaviors arise from physical or emotional needs that are unfulfilled or lacking. So it's important to make note of these areas to determine where you may be able to make changes that will address and correct any inadequacies.

1. Are you feeding your dog at least twice per day? A hungry dog is an unhappy dog. Frequency is just as important as regularity. Feed your dog on a regular schedule so that he knows when to expect his next meal. Routine, especially as it pertains to feeding, exercising, and potty breaks, provides a tremendous source of security. And of course, happy, secure dogs behave better.

2. Your dog requires more than a shelter from the elements. Dogs are social creatures who do not tolerate isolation well. Keeping a dog in an outdoor kennel, backyard, basement, or garage does not provide him with the human companionship necessary for good social development and mental health. Dogs who live apart from their human caretakers can develop destructive or aggressive tendencies.

> The principle behind using command training to solve problem behaviors is to teach your dog acceptable behaviors that replace the undesirable ones.

**3.** Dogs who live indoors with their human families can also suffer social isolation when they are left home alone for many hours every day. If your dog's social needs are greater than what you can provide, consider getting him a canine companion or enroll him in a doggy day care center a couple of days per week.

**4.** Dogs have strong instincts that influence their behavior. Some instincts are more potent in specific breeds. Hunting dogs have an especially strong scenting drive. Herding dogs have a desire to chase and herd animals. Guard dogs have strong protection instincts. What kind of powerful instincts does your dog possess? If he is highly scent-driven, make sure he has plenty of opportunities to do some outdoor sniffing. If he loves to run, give him opportunities to do so. If he is protective, take the time to socialize him continuously so that he can feel comfortable with strangers and develop the ability to judge human character. If you can help satisfy your dog's instincts, he won't have to fulfill them in ways that cause problems for you.

**5.** Perhaps the greatest challenge for some owners is to meet the need for exercise. High-energy dogs seem to have an unlimited source of fuel. Even though they can run all day without rest, it doesn't mean they require 12 hours of exercise every day. What they do need, however, is regular daily exercise, which means allotting a certain period of time every day to provide that. As long as your dog knows he can count on getting a workout, he will develop the patience to wait until then to unload his cache of energy. Can your dog count on a daily walk or a daily game of fetch?

## When not to Bother Your Buddy

Some dogs are more sensitive than others when it comes to being disturbed while eating or sleeping. Regardless of how your dog feels about it, it is a matter of respect to leave him alone during these times. Children should learn never to bother a sleeping or eating dog. Elderly dogs who have lost some hearing, or dogs who sleep very soundly, may snap if they are startled awake. Like a dog who bites out of pain, this reaction should not be considered an aggression problem.

There are other situations that may also cause a typically docile dog to bite. When a dog feels crowded, outnumbered, overwhelmed, or threatened, he may lash out to defend himself. Always pay attention when your dog shows signs of stress or anxiety, and be prepared to protect him from situations that make him feel vulnerable. By treating him with respect and expecting others to do so as well, he will never feel a need to defend himself with his teeth.

## NATURAL CANINE BEHAVIORS

A dog is a dog, and no amount of training is going to turn him into a human. Because of this, there are some situations that may require preventive measures or concessions to deal with problem behaviors. We cannot always change a dog's natural behavior, but we can find ways to manage it.

For example, dogs like to chew on things. When they are puppies, they do it to relieve the discomfort of teething. When they are adults, they have a craving to chew on hard things to clean their teeth. They like to chew up soft things because it satisfies their need to tear things apart, just as wild canines do when they dismember a kill. Shredding things with their teeth also helps them cope with stress. Dogs are scavengers, and this means they are always looking for food. They may get into the garbage, surf kitchen counters, or snatch an ice cream cone from an unwary child's hand. They don't do any of these things because they are naughty; they do them because they are dogs.

Even though you can solve many canine problem behaviors by teaching your dog a few new commands, you can significantly improve your chances of success if you remove temptations from his environment whenever possible. Put shoes and toys away so that he can't chew on them, and give him plenty of appropriate toys to meet his chewing needs. Don't leave food on your kitchen counters, as it will only serve as a reward to encourage him to continue counter

surfing, and keep your garbage in an inaccessible place. When you have done everything you can to meet your dog's needs and prevent unwanted behaviors, you can teach him a few useful commands to help manage his behavior and give him the opportunity to develop self-control.

## REPLACING PROBLEM BEHAVIORS

A dog cannot jump while he is sitting. He cannot run while he is staying in the same place. He cannot nip at your hands if he already has a toy in his mouth. The principle behind using command training to solve canine problem behaviors is to teach your dog alternative behaviors that replace the undesirable ones. For each of the following problem behaviors, you'll find command suggestions, as well as

## House Rules

It takes a whole household to train a dog. Make sure everyone in your family is on the same page concerning behavior management. This is important not only for consistency, but also because everyone who lives in your home is a member of your dog's pack and has a significant influence on his behavior. Establishing strict house rules concerning how to address issues such as begging, jumping, and nipping will contribute greatly to having a well-mannered pet.

advice on meeting your dog's needs and preventing inappropriate behaviors.

Before seeking remedies to any problem behavior, it is important to school your dog in five basic obedience commands: *sit*, *down*, *stay*, *come*, and *heel*, which are covered in Chapter 7. This will give him a chance to learn some self-control while giving you a chance to become skilled in the use of four basic communication words: *yes!*, *good*, *okay*, *uh-uh*. These cue words will help you establish your position of control and give you and your dog the confidence you need to succeed.

## COMMON PROBLEM BEHAVIORS

It doesn't matter if you've owned dogs your whole life or if this is your first rodeo.

Just when you think you know everything there is to know about dogs, one will come along to prove you wrong! This means that each individual will present his own unique challenges, and sometimes it may take some creativity to resolve his particular issues.

That being said, there are several problem behaviors that are relatively common. Remedies for them have been tried and tested for many years by numerous trainers and dog owners. The most effective methods involve a multifaceted approach—they will meet the

**You can significantly improve your dog's chances for success with training if you remove temptations from his environment whenever possible.**

dog's needs, communicate expectations, and provide an acceptable alternative behavior. The following solutions should help you deal with the most frequently encountered challenges.

## Barking

Barking is a form of communication, so pay attention to what your dog is trying to tell you. He may be trying to warn you about a stranger coming to your door. He may be trying to let you know he wants something—he wants to play, he wants to eat, or he wants to go for a walk. He may simply be barking as a plea for attention. When you understand your dog's motives for barking, you can respond to him appropriately.

1. Some of the commands you might use to address your dog's barking include *it's nothing*, *quiet*, or *who's here?*, which are covered in Chapter 9. When your dog barks to alert you to a potential threat, use the cue word *good* to encourage his good performance as a watchdog. When you consistently respond to his barking, he is less likely to do it frivolously and annoyingly because he'll realize it has a purpose.

2. If your dog has a habit of barking in your absence, he may be doing it in an

> The first step in solving problem barking is to identify the cause. Your dog may be issuing a warning or it may just be a plea for attention.

effort to relieve the stress of separation anxiety. In this case, you'll need to address his need for stress relief. If food-stuffed toys are not enough to keep him occupied, you may need to provide other activities or make other arrangements for him, such as enrolling him in a doggy day care facility or providing a canine companion for him. (See this chapter's Separation Anxiety section for more guidance on managing this issue.)

## Begging

Begging is a natural behavior for the scavenging canine. However, that doesn't mean you need to put up with a dog who drools on your shoes every time you sit down to eat. There are a few things you need to do to ensure success in breaking this annoying habit.

1. First, don't allow anyone to share their food with your dog during mealtimes. A single tidbit slipped under the table is enough to firmly establish the habit of begging! Prevention consists of eliminating any rewards your dog may get out of this behavior.

2. In addition, it helps to prohibit any type of interaction with your dog at mealtimes—do not pet him, talk to him, or look at him. When your dog accepts the fact that he won't get any attention during mealtimes, he'll accept the fact that he won't get any food, either. He will have an easier time complying with these conditions if he is not aching with hunger, so feed him at least a half hour before you sit down to dinner. When you meet your dog's needs, he won't have to meet his own needs by begging.

3. The pivotal command to turn your mendicant canine into an unobtrusive observer at dinnertime is *place*, which you can find in Chapter 9. Use the training techniques for this command to teach your dog where his proper place is during mealtimes. Choose a location within sight of your dinner table—underneath the table is fine—and consistently make him stay there when you are eating. If you already use the *place* command to send your dog to his bed or mat, use an alternate word to name his dinner place, like *spot*. Eventually, it will become a habit for him to settle down there whenever you sit down to eat.

## Destructive Chewing

There are plenty of preventives on the market to discourage dogs from chewing on inappropriate items. You can purchase a bitter-tasting spray to use on your furnishings or dab a bit of economical but potentially staining hot sauce on items your dog likes to chomp on. In either case, a preventive can help treat the symptom, but it won't solve the problem.

1. Provide a variety of toys to satisfy your dog's need to chew. Select items that are hard and soft, with a variety of textures. You'll begin to learn what types of things he favors, and when you give him what he craves, his chew toys will outshine any chair leg or end table in the house.

2. Make it easy for your dog to give up his chewing fetish by putting anything he

shouldn't be chomping on away where he can't get to it. Shoes belong in a closet. Children's toys belong in a toy bin. Dirty clothes belong in a hamper. And make sure you keep your dog's chew toys in a regular location so that he knows where to find them. A shoebox can make a great doggy toy box!

3. If you catch your dog chewing on the wrong things, tell him *uh-uh* firmly, and then give him the *get your toy* command (see Chapter 11). By doing this, you redirect him to something more appropriate. The benefit of teaching this command is that you are not simply giving him a replacement item to play with; you are teaching him to seek out and get his own toys. If he gets in the habit of getting them whenever he has an urge to chew, he won't be so inclined to grab the nearest inappropriate object.

Dogs dig for a number of reasons, but the most common is because they are bored and want something to do.

## Digging

Some dogs are natural diggers, but crater-sized holes in the lawn do absolutely nothing for a yard's aesthetic

appeal. If your dog goes overboard in his efforts to aerate your lawn, you'll need to address the situation with alternate activities, supervision, and communication. Dogs dig for a number of reasons, but the most common is because they are bored and want something to do.

1. Provide your dog with some durable, weather-resistant outdoor toys—toys that are always kept outside to provide entertainment, stimulation, and exercise. Just like indoor toys, keep these items in a central location so your dog knows where to find them.

2. Obviously, you cannot stop your dog's digging if you are not around when he digs. Supervise him closely when he's outside, and issue a firm *uh-uh* if you catch him in the act. Teach *leave it* (from Chapter 9), *get your toy*, and *fetch* (from Chapter 11) to get him to stop excavating and start focusing on a different activity.

If your dog has housetraining lapses or suddenly seems to forget his training, it may be due to a medical issue, stress, or inadequate potty breaks.

3. If your dog is of a breed that has a strong natural instinct to dig, like some terriers, consider constructing a sandbox somewhere in your yard

dedicated specifically to this purpose. Hide toys or biscuits in the sand for him to find. He'll soon decide that it's his favorite place to dig.

## House Soiling

If, despite your best efforts, your dog still has housetraining lapses, or he suddenly seems to forget his training, you must first determine a cause for the house soiling before you can find a cure. The following questions and solutions will help guide you in the right direction toward solving the problem.

1. Have you followed the housetraining instructions in this book carefully and consistently? If so, your dog should have little opportunity to have accidents in the house or to develop bad habits. If not, start from the beginning and retrain your dog using stricter controls to prevent mistakes on both your parts.

2. Are your expectations realistic? Some dogs take longer to housetrain than others. In fact, many small breeds are known to take an exceptionally long time to housetrain (up to a year!), so be sure to give your dog the benefit of the doubt. If you recently adopted a dog who should already be housetrained, allow him a couple months to adjust to his new home and schedule. Meanwhile, take precautions to prevent accidents by restricting his space inside your home and supervising him closely.

3. Could there be a medical reason for your dog's behavior? House soiling may be caused by urinary tract infections, incontinence, or other physical conditions. If your dog was previously housetrained and suddenly starts having lapses, take him to the veterinarian to rule out possible health issues.

4. Does your dog have a dominant personality? Dominant dogs like to do things their own way, and this may include house soiling for the simple reason that it is more convenient than going outside. In this case, food rewards can make it more worthwhile for your dog to do his business outside. When praise isn't enough, do not hesitate to step up the reward.

5. Are you expecting your dog to hold it too long? Puppies, in particular, have small bladders and need to urinate frequently. Make sure your dog is getting adequate potty breaks at regular intervals. If you need to be gone for a long period of time, make arrangements for someone else to take him outside.

6. Is your dog on a regular eating, sleeping, and activity schedule? These three things regulate a dog's entire system and can contribute to regularity in his elimination habits. If you observe him carefully, you'll get to know what times of day he usually needs to go outside.

## Jumping

Jumping can be a perplexing problem because it is so self-rewarding; it is a perfect way for an excitable dog to release some of his excess energy. Puppies are notorious for leaping about when they are excited, and this can be an especially challenging age to deal with a jumper. They do not have much self-control, and their jumping tends to persist no matter what training methods their owners use to combat the behavior. Nonetheless, it is important to be consistent and persistent in discouraging jumping, even in adults. Believe it or not, your instruction will eventually sink in.

1. Jumping really is a personal space issue, and your efforts to eradicate this behavior have a better chance for success if your dog respects you. If he does not respect your judgment or wishes, he probably won't respect your personal space, either. So make sure you practice good canine leadership skills. And of course, always tell your dog *good* when he respects your personal space and keeps his paws to himself.

2. For adult dogs, teaching the cue words *off* (from Chapter 9) and *sit* (from Chapter 7) can effectively prevent jumping. Use these commands consistently whenever your dog is prone to jump, such as when he greets people or when you play with him.

3. For puppies or high-energy dogs who find it impossible to sit because they are bursting with too much energy, teach *get your toy* (from Chapter 11) so that they can release energy in an appropriate way. After giving this command, play with your dog for a minute or two before you ask him to sit for a greeting.

## Leash Pulling

If dogs could tell us their biggest complaint about humans, they would probably say we are too slow. In many cases, leash pulling is a self-rewarding behavior because the dog does indeed get to go faster by dragging his owner down the street. So the most important part of resolving this problem behavior is to take the reward out of it.

1. The instructions for the *walk nice* command in Chapter 10 outline how to accomplish this. The technique of stopping or reversing direction each time your dog pulls will soon teach him that pulling does not give him what he wants—that is, it doesn't allow him to go faster. In fact, it doesn't allow him to go anywhere at all. But when you reward him with the opportunity to move forward each time he puts slack back in the leash, he will soon learn to adjust his speed of travel to match yours.

2. One of the secrets to successful leash training, believe it or not, is *not* to take your dog for walks until he *is* leash trained. If you walk your dog some distance away from home and attempt to train him along the way, you may eventually realize you'll never get home again if you keep stopping or reversing direction. You may then end up allowing him to pull in order to get home before dark. Each time you reward your dog by allowing him to pull, the behavior becomes more deeply ingrained. So keep your training sessions very close to home, and save longer walks for when his leash training is complete. The best way to get rid of a bad habit is not to let it develop in the first place!

3. Train your dog not to pull right from the start. If he needs to develop more self-discipline in regard to his leash

skills, consider teaching him the more disciplined *heel* command in Chapter 7. And as always, keep your expectations realistic. If you have a high-energy dog, practice Exercise First from Chapter 4 prior to your walks to help him succeed.

## Nipping

Nipping and mouthing are common behaviors for puppies and young dogs, but they are also painful and annoying to humans.

1. You need to let your dog know that you do not appreciate these behaviors with a firm *uh-uh*. Then withdraw your attention and ignore him until he calms down. These time-outs may be enough to convince him to keep his teeth off you,

but if you want to redirect him to more bite-appropriate items, consider teaching him the *get your toy*, *fetch*, or *pull* commands from Chapter 11.

> By stopping or reversing direction each time your dog pulls, he will soon learn that the behavior will not give him what he wants—the reward of going faster has been removed.

2. With consistent enforcement of the no-nipping rule, most dogs eventually outgrow this behavior. A few, however, continue to mouth their owner's hands, bite at their leashes, or use their mouths in other inappropriate ways into adulthood. This can be a sign of disrespect and defiance, and it's up to you to make it

clear to your dog that you expect him to treat you with respect. Make sure that you are practicing good canine leadership skills, and practice some of the power commands regularly to get your point across.

## Medical Causes for Problem Behaviors

Although problem behaviors are often rooted in a dog's natural instincts and require training to resolve, they may also be caused by a variety of medical conditions that require professional intervention:

- Housetraining lapses can be the result of urinary tract infections or obstructions. If your dog dribbles urine, urinates while sleeping, or urinates frequently, have him examined by your veterinarian.
- Nipping may be a sign of pain, especially if this behavior is out of character for your dog. A veterinary checkup may be able to determine the source of the pain.
- Aggression or fearfulness can be caused by thyroid dysfunction. Watch for other symptoms, such as hair loss or unusual weight gain, and take your dog to the veterinarian if you suspect his behavior may be health related.

## Running Away

Dogs who run away (especially in the case of younger dogs) are typically expressing their need to sniff and hunt, find a mate, or get adequate exercise. If you want your dog to be a loyal homebody rather than a roving Casanova, the first thing you must do is have him surgically sterilized, which will eliminate the production of hormones responsible for roaming behavior.

1. If your dog is of the hunting or scenting type, give him regular opportunities to do some sniffing. Take daily walks and let him stop to sniff about occasionally. Take him to the park at least once a week, and let him cast about on the end of a long line to pick up scents. Hiking trails, with their abundance of wildlife scent trails, are ideal places to meet these needs. When you give your dog opportunities to satisfy his scenting instincts, he may very well decide it is much more fun to go sniffing *with* you than to run off *without* you. Dogs are, after all, pack animals, and they much prefer to travel in a group than to go it alone.

2. If your dog is the high-energy type, you'll need to meet his need for exercise before you can get him to stop running. In addition to a daily regimen of physically demanding exercise, like a game of fetch or practice on an agility course, a daily walk can meet requirements for mental stimulation and exploration. When you have first addressed your dog's needs, he will be much more likely to learn and respond to the *come* command reliably.

Teach *come* (see Chapter 7) in many different situations and locations so that your dog will respond to it anywhere. The importance of instilling complete obedience to this command cannot be overstated, as the consequences for noncompliance can be severe. Dogs who run away can become lost, injured, or even killed. But your dog is not the only one who faces consequences—you may face fines or other penalties if he runs at large.

Until your runaway responds reliably to *come*, it is in you and your dog's best interest to take precautions to prevent him from escaping. Keep him on a leash or in a fenced area when he is outdoors, and make sure he is always supervised. To prevent him from slipping out of the house when people are coming and going, and to keep him from jumping out of the car before you can get a leash on him, teach him the *wait* command from Chapter 9.

> Dogs who run away are typically expressing their need to sniff and hunt, find a mate, or get adequate exercise.

3. It requires a lot of diligent work and training before a dog responds reliably to the *come* command, and you'll need to constantly reinforce this training throughout your dog's life. Until you have thoroughly trained him to come when called, there are a few tricks you can use to retrieve him if he decides to go AWOL. Teach him the *treat* and *ride* commands

(from Chapter 9) or *let's go!* (from Chapter 10) so that you can use them to entice him to come to you. Just be sure to deliver a treat, walk, or ride if he does.

4. In some cases, it helps to let your dog burn off some energy by allowing him to explore for a while before attempting to retrieve him. Walk parallel to him to prevent chasing him farther away, and when he's had a chance to wander a bit, attempt to get him to follow you with the *this way* command from Chapter 10. Your dog may be more than willing to chase after you if you run away from him while clapping and calling to him.

## Separation Anxiety

The primary reason dogs make such great companions for humans is because they are extremely social animals. It is natural for them to live in a family group, regardless of whether that family comprises canines or people. Dogs develop very close bonds to their pack members, and they contribute their own dynamics to that social group. Unfortunately, these strong relationships can also create a condition called "separation anxiety" in dogs who have difficulty being separated from their group members.

In this modern, demanding world, it's impossible for most owners to spend

Because they develop very close bonds to their pack members, dogs can suffer social isolation and separation anxiety if they are left home alone for many hours every day.

every moment of every day with their pets, so Fido often needs to spend some time on his own. Although many dogs adapt quite well to being alone for periods of time, some suffer acute anxiety. This condition may be expressed in different ways, but the most common are house soiling, barking, and destructive activities.

Though a number of factors may contribute to these behaviors, personality is a likely component. High-strung or high-energy dogs may be more susceptible to separation anxiety. If they have been left alone often or have suffered bad experiences or trauma, they may also be more prone to this problem. Fortunately, there are ways to address or manage it.

1. A newly adopted dog may show signs of separation anxiety, such as following his human around constantly and whining or barking if she leaves the room, even for just a few minutes. This type of separation anxiety is often borne of insecurity due to the loss of his previous home; instability of his schedule; and being moved around to vet clinics, shelters, or foster homes. Sometimes, all it takes is a little time for the dog to adjust to his new surroundings and regain a sense of security. Patience is usually the only remedy needed.

2. More serious forms of separation anxiety call for help in the form of behavior modification and/ or environmental concessions. A consultation with a professional animal behaviorist may be in order so that you can determine the cause,

the triggers that affect it, and the best ways to approach helping your dog. Behavior modification may include mock departures—pretending to leave by putting on a coat and getting your keys—to desensitize him to separation rituals. Diversions may include providing him with a companion dog, leaving him with

## Senior Moments

Advanced age brings with it many physiological changes in dogs, just as it does in people. These changes can contribute to canine behaviors that, on the surface, appear to be problem behaviors like aggression, disobedience, or house soiling. Arthritis pain may cause an older dog to be irritable, nippy, or reluctant to move. Loss of hearing may cause him to ignore commands. Incontinence, renal failure, and digestive upset can all contribute to housetraining lapses. Cognitive dysfunction can cause an older dog to forget his training or become lost or confused easily. Many of these age-related conditions are responsive to medical treatment, and others can be managed. If your senior appears to develop a problem behavior, a veterinary checkup is in order to look for health causes.

a treat-filled toy to keep him busy while you are gone, or even providing soothing music or white noise to keep him calm in your absence. Doggy day care is always an option for dogs who need more social contact than their owners can provide.

3. Other helpful actions include removing targets of destruction from your dog's environment, using bitter spray repellents to discourage him from damaging property, or confining him to a pet-safe room while you are gone.

Separation anxiety can be a perplexing problem to solve, so it's in your best interest to avoid contributing to this condition. Always keep your departures and arrivals as low key as possible and avoid fussing over your dog when you are coming and going. Keeping him on a regular feeding and exercise schedule will contribute greatly to his sense of security and confidence, and this, in turn, helps to keep anxiety levels low.

## SERIOUS PROBLEM BEHAVIORS

Some problem behaviors require more than command training, leadership, prevention, and effective communication to solve. Canines are complicated creatures who use their own brand of psychology to govern their behavior. You cannot expect to have the knowledge and experience necessary to deal with every canine behavioral challenge, but it's important to be able to recognize when you are not equipped to handle a problem on your own. It also helps to know where to go when you need advice and guidance.

## A Word of Caution About Aggression

One of the most daunting of canine problem behaviors is aggression, of which there are several different types. Some dogs are aggressive only toward other dogs. Some are fence-line (territorially) aggressive, and some express dominance aggression through their possessiveness over food dishes, toys, furniture, or people. Due to the danger of injury to humans, seek specialized help for any of these types of problems.

This particular canine problem behavior is so serious that even a professional dog trainer may not be able to handle it. You may have to enlist the services of someone who has specific experience and expertise in this area because the wrong solution can make aggression problems worse. Consulting with a certified animal behaviorist is usually the best plan of action. You can find qualified professionals through the International Association of Animal Behavior Consultants (IAABC) website at www.iaabc.org or the American Veterinary Society of Animal Behavior (AVSAB) website at www.avsabonline.org.

Problem behaviors that you can't seem to solve by meeting your dog's needs and providing consistent training may have deeper causes. Since medical problems can contribute to undesirable behavior, it may help to have a veterinarian rule out physical causes. If your dog receives a clean bill of health, the problem may be more psychological than physical, in which case you may need the assistance of a professional dog trainer or animal behaviorist.

## Professional Assistance

Dogs who have exceptionally strong instincts can develop difficult-to-manage and dangerous behaviors like car chasing. High-strung dogs may be prone to the frustrating and perplexing problem of advanced separation anxiety, which may be challenging to resolve. Still others may develop obsessive-compulsive disorders or other psychological issues for which training is not sufficient.

High-energy dogs may be more prone to separation anxiety.

Do not hesitate to consult a professional dog trainer or animal behaviorist if a problem behavior is resistant to your efforts to correct it. Contact local animal shelters or veterinarians for reliable referrals. Some animal shelters have animal behaviorists on staff who can provide advice at little or no cost. The Association of Pet Dog Trainers (APDT) has a directory of certified dog trainers on its website at www.apdt.com, as does the National Association of Dog Obedience Instructors (NADOI) at www.nadoi.org.

# PART THREE

## TRAINING

## COMMANDS

# 7

# OBEDIENCE COMMANDS

Obedience training is a term that can refer to any type of training that requires a dog to be compliant to his handler's commands. However, the connotations associated with this term include commands that yield the greatest amount of control, those that necessitate absolute compliance, and those associated with obedience trials. For the purposes of this book, we'll have to narrow down this definition. The commands covered in this chapter are basic obedience commands, most of which are required for novice obedience trials as defined by the American Kennel Club (AKC). These are the most important commands you can teach, as they represent the minimum amount of control you need to possess to have a well-mannered dog.

Think of basic obedience training as your dog's elementary education. Many of the instructions in this book require one or more basic obedience commands as prerequisites. And indeed, virtually all dog sports require a foundation in basic obedience before qualifying to train in other advanced disciplines.

The time and effort you put into teaching your dog obedience skills is always worth the investment. Besides providing him with good manners, it gives you the opportunity to establish a line of communication with him and accustom him to learning,

> Obedience training is a term that can refer to any type of training that requires a dog to be compliant to his handler's commands.

which is the greatest gift you can give him. And if you do this right, with positive reinforcement and encouragement, you may very well teach him to love learning as well. Then you can help your canine best friend reach his true potential.

## COME (ALSO: HERE, COME HERE)

### Description
The dog comes within reach of his handler.

### Uses
This command is useful in so many situations that it is impossible to list them all. Because your dog needs to know this command for you to keep him safe, it is the single most important one you can teach him.

### Prerequisites
None.

### Training Technique
In the interest of communicating effectively with your dog, choose one command word for this skill and stick to it. Too often, people use a variety of expressions to instruct their dogs to come to them, such as "come here," "come here, I mean it," "get your butt over here," or "if you don't come here right now…" Most of the time, these phrases are issued in an irritated tone of voice, which effectively discourages most dogs from coming.

In addition, remember that the purpose of your dog's name is to get his attention, not to instruct him to come. If

someone were to call your name, you would probably say, "What?" Your dog should respond to his name the same way. He should look at you to find out what you want of him.

> A reliable *recall* is the most important skill you can teach your dog.

The *come* command is inherently important because a dog who does not come when his owner calls him can become lost, hit by a car, poisoned, or worse. This is why you should begin to regularly practice come as soon as you acquire a new pet. Most dogs take a while to respond to the *come* command consistently, so be sure to take precautions to prevent your dog from running off—keep him on a leash, a long line, or in a fenced area when outdoors.

When a dog learns to respond consistently to the *come* command, he has a reliable "recall." To develop a reliable *recall*, there are a few rules you should always follow:

1. Always issue the *come* command in a positive, upbeat manner.
2. Never call your dog to come to you if it will result in an unpleasant experience for him, such as a bath, a trip to the vet, or confinement. (In these cases, always go get him rather than calling him to you.)
3. Most importantly, never punish your dog when he comes to you, even if he did not come when you initially called him. This is a surefire way to discourage him from coming the next time you call him.

Instead, use a variety of training techniques in the home, in a fenced area, and on a long line to help establish a reliable *recall*.

## In the Home
It's easiest to begin training *come* indoors.

1. Keep some treats in your pocket or place them in several locations around your home so that you can access them easily. Wait until your dog is distracted or occupied, and then call his name and give the *come* command.
2. Each time your dog responds

**Begin teaching the *come* command with your dog on leash, and always reward him for coming when you call him.**

to this command, issue a *yes!* and reward him with a treat and plenty of praise. To heighten his sensitivity to this command, say it only once each time. If he does not respond immediately, he will miss out on a yummy treat.

## In a Fenced Area

The outdoors provides greater distractions to challenge your dog. If you have a safe, fenced area in which to practice, this is an ideal environment to improve reliability.

1. Wait until your dog is distracted, and then call his name and give the *come* command. Encourage him to come to you by calling him in a happy voice, clapping your hands, slapping your thighs, squatting down, or running away from him. (Dogs love to play chase.)
2. If your dog comes, give him an enthusiastic *yes!* and reward him with a treat. Again, call him only once each time.

## On a Long Line

Regardless of whether or not you have a fenced outdoor area in which to practice, training with a long line offers its own advantages. It can keep your dog safe while working in a variety of outdoor locations to further improve his reliability. Long leashes or tracking lines are sold at many pet supply stores, but an inexpensive cotton clothesline attached securely to his collar can work just as well. (Avoid nylon lines, as they can cause rope burns if your dog becomes entangled in them.)

## Reliable Recalls

There are times when all the praise in the world may not be as desirable as chasing a squirrel or rabbit, especially for a hunting breed. Breeds like Alaskan Malamutes and Greyhounds are simply born to run. A truly reliable *recall* may be unrealistic for some dogs; however, a great many develop an amazing amount of self-control over their powerful instincts. They listen to their owners for one reason only— because they respect and trust them. Achieving a reliable *recall* depends just as much on mental control as it does on training. So if your dog has considerable difficulty learning the *come* command, make sure he accepts you as a trustworthy and reliable canine leader, as described in Chapter 3.

1. Let your dog explore some distance away from you while on the long line, and then call his name and give the *come* command.
2. If your dog responds, say the cue word *yes!* and reward him with a treat. It's very important to avoid pulling him to you if he does not obey. You do not want to teach him that you are in control only when he is on a leash or line. The purpose of the long line is to keep him safe, not to force him to come to you.

3. When your dog comes to you consistently while on a long line, you can finally attempt to give him a little more freedom. Drop the long line on the ground, and let him explore at his leisure with the line dragging behind him. This way, if he does decide to ignore your *come* command, you can easily catch him by running after him and stepping on the end of the line.

4. If you haven't already started to phase out food rewards, this is the time to do it. You can begin to replace them with effusive praise or playtime with a favorite toy. In any case, there should always be something good waiting for your dog when he comes to you. You can condition him to respond to come to you automatically if you always make it beneficial for him.

## COME 'ROUND (ALSO: GO 'ROUND, SWING)

### Description
From a *front* position (standing or sitting, facing his handler), the dog goes to the left side of his handler and turns around into a *heel* position.

### Uses
This skill helps your dog perform a smooth transition from a *front* position into a *heel* position. It is useful in many different training disciplines, including obedience sports and canine musical freestyle.

### Prerequisites
*Front* and *heel*.

### Training Technique
In this maneuver, your dog turns in toward you when he turns around, so he needs to learn to leave enough space between himself and you so that he can execute this move smoothly.

1. Start with your dog in a sitting or standing *front* position. Then lure him with a treat so that he walks to your left side and swings toward you as he turns around. His head should end up by your left knee (*heel* position).

2. When your dog completes this maneuver, issue a *yes!* and reward him with the treat. When he begins to execute this move smoothly, start using the *come 'round* command whenever you want him to perform it. You can also start making your luring motions more subtle so that they evolve into a less conspicuous hand signal. Eventually, you want to be able to signal your dog to come 'round with a slight circular motion of your finger rather than luring him with a treat.

3. Like other obedience commands, phase out treats gradually. Do not mislead your dog into thinking obedience is a paid job. Gradually replace the food with ample praise to strengthen his desire to please you.

## DOWN (ALSO: LIE DOWN)

### Description
The dog lies down on his stomach.

### Uses
The *down* is a starting position for many tricks and other skills. It is also a

good replacement behavior for certain problems, such as barking and begging. (It is less comfortable for a dog to bark while lying down than while standing, and a begging dog is less likely to be a pest if he is lying down.) This skill comes in handy if you want to get your dog to remain in a particular spot—he can't move around very easily on his stomach. It is also a safe and comfortable position for him to maintain while riding in a vehicle.

## Prerequisites
*Sit.*

## Training Technique
Most dogs learn this skill easier in stages. Be prepared to reward your dog for every little bit of progress he makes.

1. Ask your dog to do a *sit* in front of you, and then attempt to lure him into a *down* position with a treat. Hold the treat on the floor in front of him, and when he is fixated on it, slowly draw it away from him so that he stretches out to get it.

2. If your dog inches his front feet forward just a little bit while keeping his rear end planted, issue an immediate *yes!* and let him have the treat.

3. Gradually ask your dog to stretch out more and more before you give him a

The *down* command is a prerequisite for many other skills and tricks, but it is most useful in getting your dog to settle or remain in position when necessary.

*yes!* and a reward. He will eventually begin to drop his front end all the way to the floor. If he stands up during the training process, you may be trying to progress too fast. Take your time. It may take several training sessions before he rests his elbows on the floor in a full *down* position. When he does, plenty of enthusiastic praise is in order.

4. When your dog has achieved a full *down* position, you may start using the *down* command for this skill. Then instead of luring him into this position with a treat, you can begin to point to the ground in front of him when you instruct him to lie down. You want to gradually mold this gesture into the traditional hand signal for *down*, which consists of a flat hand, palm down, moving downward from your chest to your stomach (as if you are pushing down on something).

5. As with all obedience commands, phase out food rewards for this skill and get your dog in the habit of obeying this command without such incentives. This, of course, does not mean there are no rewards for good manners. Praise and petting are always acceptable for good behavior. Don't forget to use the cue word *good* whenever your dog pleases you, and provide consistent, firm leadership so that he will work hard to meet your expectations.

## FOOS

### Description

Although the word "foos" (sounds like "loose") means *heel* in German, foreign language instruction is not required! This command instructs the dog to walk close to his handler's right side (the opposite side from *heel*).

### Uses

This right-side *heel* position is useful any time the typical left-side *heel* position is impractical, such as when walking two dogs at the same time. It is also a common position in the sport of canine musical freestyle, where the dog needs to occupy different positions around his handler.

### Prerequisites

*Sit.*

### Training Technique

The training technique for *foos* is the same as that used for *heel* except that the position is reversed. You will hold the leash in your left hand while your dog walks on your right side.

1. Start with your dog in a sitting position at your right side. Give the *foos* command as you begin to walk, and hold a treat at your right side to encourage him to maintain his position there.

2. If your dog remains in a *foos* position for just a few steps, issue a *yes!* and reward him. If he moves too far ahead of the *foos* position, stop and start over with him in a sitting position at your right side.

3. When your dog consistently performs a *foos* for a few steps, begin to increase the number of steps you ask him to foos before you reward him.

Once he has the hang of it, begin using your right hand to pat the side of your right leg instead of holding a treat there—this will become your hand signal to tell him to foos. Deliver the treats from your left hand during this phase of training.

4. Like other obedience commands, your dog eventually needs to perform this command without food incentives. When he is proficient at *foos*, begin phasing out the food rewards and replace them with praise and the cue word *good*.

## FRONT

### Description
The dog comes and sits directly in front of his handler.

### Uses
This maneuver is useful in a number of training disciplines, including obedience, rally obedience, and canine musical freestyle. It puts your dog in a good position to receive further instructions from you.

The *front* command puts your dog in a seated position in front of you so that he can receive further instructions.

### Prerequisites
*Sit*, *stay*, and *come*.

### Training Technique
A dog who has mastered all of the prerequisites for this command already possesses the skills needed to perform a *front*. This command means, "come

and sit in front of me." Teaching it to your dog simply requires performing the prerequisite skills in the necessary order: *sit*, *stay*, *come*, and *sit*.

1. With your dog in the *sit* position, give the *stay* command and then walk a short distance away from your dog.
2. Call your dog with a *come* command while holding a treat in each hand, arms outstretched in front of you. This is to encourage him to approach you straight on. (Later, these hand positions will evolve into a hand signal that consists of holding your hands in front of you with your flat palms facing each other, as if you were holding a box by the sides.)
3. When your dog reaches you, give the *sit* command. If he responds appropriately, issue a *yes!* and reward him.
4. When your dog is proficient in exercising this sequence of commands, begin using the *front* command instead of the *come* and *sit* commands.
5. Finally, begin using the aforementioned hand signal instead of holding treats in your hands. Continue to deliver food rewards until your dog responds consistently to this command. Like other obedience commands, you need to slowly phase them out after he has mastered this skill. Replace the food rewards with praise and the cue word *good*.

## HEEL

### Description
The dog walks at his handler's left side, with his head close to his handler's leg.

### Uses
The *heel* command is a required skill for obedience competition. It is a way to keep a leashed or unleashed dog under control. It requires more precision and discipline than *walk nice* (from Chapter 10), but you can teach it in addition to and independently of *walk nice*. It is an excellent skill to teach a dog who likes to pull on the leash. As a form of movement control, this is a very valuable power command.

### Prerequisites
*Sit*.

### Training Technique
Alternative to the following training instructions, you can use the training technique for *walk nice* to accomplish a

### Don't Overuse Your Dog's Name
The *look* command is used in many different training disciplines to get a dog's attention, but consider the fact that you may often use your dog's name to serve the same purpose. It is preferable to have him respond with eager attention to his name. However, if it is overused and he is not very sensitive to it, *look* provides a good alternative.

*heel*. The difference is simply expecting your dog to maintain a disciplined position at your left side, with his head near your left leg rather than just keeping slack in the leash.

1. Begin with your dog sitting at your left side. Hold the leash in your right hand, with any excess leash coiled loosely.
2. Issue the *heel* command, and lure your dog to walk close to your left side holding a treat in your left hand. Take only two or three steps.
3. If your dog maintains a *heel* position, issue a *yes!* and give him the treat.
4. Repeat the above steps. As your dog shows proficiency in heeling for just a few steps, increase the number of steps you take before issuing a *yes!* and rewarding him.
5. When your dog understands what you expect whenever you ask for the *heel*, you are ready to fade out the food rewards for this skill. When you are no longer using food to motivate his compliance, you must make it clear to him that you still expect him to obey. Nurture his natural will to please by using the cue word

For his safety as well as yours, your dog needs to learn to stay on one side of you during walks. The *heel* command helps to keep him under control—whether he is leashed or unleashed.

*good* whenever he performs the *heel* appropriately.

6. When your dog heels well on leash, try heeling off leash. (If he is not proficient in the *come* command, practice this in a safe, fenced area or indoors.) Be prepared to use food to lure him into position if necessary, as you will not have a leash to correct or guide him. Once he performs this skill reliably off leash, you can then fade the food rewards as you did for the on-leash lessons.

## LOOK (ALSO: LOOK AT ME, WATCH, WATCH ME)

### Description
The dog looks at and pays attention to his handler.

### Uses
Although this isn't technically an obedience command, it can assist greatly in obedience training because it can help you communicate with your dog. It is difficult to expect him to comply with your obedience commands if you do not first have his attention when instructing him. Use *look* to interrupt his focus on other things and direct his attention to you prior to issuing any command.

### Prerequisites
None.

### Training Technique
1. Lure your dog's attention to your face by waving a treat in front of his face,

and then bring the treat up to your forehead. Give the *look* command enthusiastically when you do this.

> Use *look* to direct your dog's attention to you prior to issuing any command.

2. When your dog looks at your face, issue a *yes!* and reward him.
3. After your dog gets in the habit of looking at your face, you should no longer have to lure him with the treat; just hold it up to your forehead when you say, "Look."
4. With practice, your dog will begin to look at your face, even when you are not holding a treat there. Continue to reward

him for his correct responses until the behavior becomes well established.

# SIT

## Description
The dog sits down.

## Uses
This command is one of the foundations of canine control. The *sit* is useful for teaching your dog many other skills that begin with a sitting position, including obedience commands like *down* and *stay*. It is also a good alternative behavior to use so that he won't jump up on you. You can use it to immobilize him and keep him from chasing animals, bicycles, or cars. It can also help with dominance or excessive barking behaviors because a sitting dog cannot display a dominant or aggressive/alert posture.

## Prerequisites
None.

## Training Technique
Sitting is a very natural, comfortable position for a dog, so most dogs pick this skill up fairly easily. In fact, even dogs who seem to know little else tend to know the *sit* command.

1. With your dog in front of you, hold a treat in front of him, and draw it slowly over his head so that he has to look up to see it. Do not hold it so high

> Teaching your dog to sit will keep him from chasing animals and vehicles.

The *sit* is useful for teaching your dog many other commands, like *down* and *stay*.

that he jumps up to get it. Instead, hold it within his reach, but keep your hand closed around it so he can't get it.

2. By the time you have drawn the treat over your dog's head, just above his eye level, he may have automatically backed up into a *sit* in order to keep his eyes on it. If so, issue a *yes!* and reward him. If not, you can assist him into a *sit* by practicing this skill on leash and gently pulling it in a diagonal upward-backward direction, which will help lift his front end and encourage his back end to drop. If he successfully performs a *sit*, issue a *yes!* and reward him.

3. As soon as your dog learns to sit

down when you hold a treat over his head, you can start to use the *sit* command. Issue a *sit* before you lure him into the position with a treat, and as he becomes proficient at it, begin to fade out the food rewards. You can also teach him a hand signal for *sit* by gradually adjusting your luring motions until you are raising your fist as if you are lifting a dumbbell, or you can get in the habit of pointing to his rear end when you tell him to sit.

## STAY

### Description
The dog stays in his place (sitting, standing, or lying down).

### Uses
Like other movement-control commands, this is a power command. Use it to prevent your dog from chasing animals or going out the door when people are coming and going. It is a prerequisite for many other commands like *get back*, *in*, *leash on*, and *load up* (which are found in Chapter 10). Also use it to prevent your dog from breaking a command like *sit* or *down* until you give him the cue word *okay*.

### Prerequisites
*Sit*, *stand*, or *down* (depending on the position you want your dog to hold).

### Training Technique
Don't underestimate the power of this command; it can give you considerable control over your dog. Take the time to

train him thoroughly in *stay*, and practice it often.

1. For the *sit/stay*, tell your dog to perform a *sit* in front of you, and then give the *stay* command. Take one step backward, and immediately step toward him again. If he has maintained his position, issue a *yes!* and reward him.

2. Keep repeating Step 1, but gradually increase the number of steps you walk away from your dog. Always walk all the way back to him before issuing a *yes!* and rewarding him. Don't give him a *stay* and then call him to come to you. This might result in your dog learning that *stay* means "stay for a little while and then come," and he'll never hold a *stay* for very long. If he keeps breaking the *stay*, you may be progressing too fast, in which case you need to shorten the amount of distance and time you expect him to remain in position.

3. With a gradual increase in the amount of distance and time you ask your dog to stay, he will eventually be able to remain stationary when you cross the entire room. Then he'll be ready to learn the out-of-sight *stay*. Give the *stay* command,

and take one step out of the room (out of your dog's range of sight). Immediately step back into the room and return to your dog. If he has maintained his position, issue a *yes!* and reward him.

4. Gradually increase the amount of time you expect your dog to remain in *stay* when you are out of sight. Soon, he will stay anchored in position for as long as you like, regardless of whether or not he can see you.

For other *stay* positions, like *stand/stay* or *down/stay*, teach your dog the position command first, then repeat these steps with him in that position.

Teaching your dog to stay in position reliably will make him more pleasant to have around and can help keep him safe in various situations.

# 8

# HANDLING COMMANDS

Imagine how difficult it would be to care for your dog if you couldn't touch him. How would you groom him? How would you administer medications? How would you help him if he got stuck in a bad situation or needed assistance getting in or out of a vehicle or up and down stairs?

Fortunately, most dogs love petting and are naturally receptive to being touched. However, there are invariably body parts that are highly sensitive, like paws, tails, and genitalia. There are also areas you may find difficult to access, like the underbelly, inside the ears, or the teeth. For your dog's own well-being, it's important for you to be able to handle him properly and safely. So take the time to train him to tolerate handling.

## BELLY UP (ALSO: SHOW YOUR BELLY, WHERE'S YOUR BELLY BUTTON?)

### Description
The dog rolls onto his back to expose his underside.

### Uses
This position makes it easy to examine or groom the underside of your dog. Also, if he learns to respond to the command *where's your belly button?*, it can become an entertaining trick. With his feet in the air, it can also become a form of play dead (see Chapter 12).

> Aside from being an entertaining trick, *belly up* makes it easy for you to groom your dog's underside.

## Prerequisites

*Down* and *stay*.

## Training Technique

One thing to keep in mind when teaching *belly up* is that this position (lying on the back) falls exactly between *play dead* (lying flat on the side) and *roll over* (rolling completely over). If you plan to also teach *play dead* and *roll over*, it is best to teach these skills in a specific order: *play dead*, *belly up*, and then *roll over*. If you attempt to teach your dog *play dead* after he has already learned *belly up*, it may be difficult to get him to lie on his side without rolling onto his back. Likewise, if you attempt to teach *belly up* after he has already learned *roll over*, it will be difficult to get him to roll onto his back without rolling completely over.

## Without Food Rewards

1. Give the *belly up* command, and then reward your dog with a delectable tummy scratching. Soon, he will roll onto his back enthusiastically to enjoy such a welcome treat.

2. When you begin to use *belly up* to assist in grooming your dog, always give him a reward of belly rubbing for his compliance before working on his underside. Then instruct him further by giving the *stay* command so that he will maintain this position for you. An occasional *good* will remind him that you are pleased with his behavior, and a special treat is in order at the end of every grooming session.

## Buddy Language: Benefits of Handling Commands

Teaching your dog handling commands not only makes it easier for you to care for him; it also helps him to feel more comfortable in a number of situations. If you show your dog, he will need to allow a judge to touch and handle his body. If he requires professional grooming, he needs to allow a groomer to handle his face, ears, feet, tail, and other body parts without nipping. An education in handling can make veterinary exams much less stressful and traumatic as well.

## With Food Rewards

1. Some dogs will learn this command quicker or perform this skill more consistently if you offer food rewards. With your dog in a *down* position, lure him into a *belly up* position with a treat. Hold the treat close to his nose, and then draw the treat over to his side so that he looks toward his flanks.

2. Slowly begin to move the treat up over his back until he begins to roll over attempting to keep his eyes on the treat. If you have trouble getting him to roll over with his belly up, reward him for smaller successes first, such as rolling onto his side, and gradually work toward a *belly up* position.

**3.** When he achieves a *belly up* position, issue an immediate *yes!* and reward him with the treat. Timing is important here, as you do not want your dog to roll over completely. It may help to place your hand on his belly to prevent him from moving any farther once he has reached the correct position. Eventually, he will understand exactly how far you expect him to roll. Then you can begin to use the *belly up* command so that he can associate it with the *belly up* position.

## EARS (ALSO: MOUTH, EYES, FEET)

### Description

These words prepare the dog to have his various body parts handled.

### Uses

Letting your dog know in advance that you plan to handle one of his body parts will help him feel more comfortable with it because he'll know exactly what your intentions are. These words can also help keep your dog calm and compliant during grooming and veterinary visits.

> *Easy* can help calm your dog whenever he gets overly excited, nervous, or impatient.

### Prerequisites

None.

### Training Technique

**1.** When handling and grooming your dog, use the names of the body parts you handle regularly. Say the command word right before you touch that specific part of the body. For instance, *mouth* right before you brush his teeth; *eyes* right before you remove the stains or foreign matter around his eyes; *ears* right before you clean his ears; and *feet* right before you pick up his feet to inspect, wipe off, or groom them.

2. Another practice that will help your dog develop trust in handling is to groom his body parts in the same order every time. He will quickly learn what to expect and get a feel for when you are almost done. Of course, concluding each grooming session with a special treat also goes a long way toward encouraging his good behavior during grooming sessions.

Your dog will eventually become familiar with the names of his body parts and comfortably accept grooming—and he may even begin to present the body part you name for your inspection!

# EASY (ALSO: SETTLE, STEADY, RELAX)

## Description
This command instructs the dog to keep a calm composure.

## Uses
*Easy* can help calm your dog whenever he gets overly excited, nervous, or impatient. It is useful during grooming, when meeting new dogs or people, or whenever he becomes noisy, whiny, or fidgety. It also serves as a warning for him to exercise self-control when faced with a strong stimulus, helping to keep him in check so that he doesn't chase after a squirrel, cat, or strange dog.

## Prerequisites
None.

## Training Technique

1. Although you can use food rewards to teach this command, they aren't really necessary, and they may actually sabotage your training efforts, especially if food gets your dog overly excited. In fact, the purpose of the cue word *yes!* and food rewards is to get your dog excited and enthusiastic about learning, which is the opposite type of response you want to achieve with the *easy* command.

2. Instead, encourage your dog to remain calm by saying the *easy* command in a low, quiet voice and using the cue

### Desensitization

The process of desensitizing your dog to having various body parts touched can make him much more tolerant of young children, who may not understand that dogs have sensitive areas. And it is necessary training if you're considering getting involved in therapy or service work or any type of work with children, disabled persons, or the elderly. But all dogs will benefit from being well schooled in handling commands.

word *good* to let him know when he has acquired the right state of mind. With consistent use of this command in a variety of situations, he will learn what you expect of him.

# HUGS (ALSO: GIVE ME HUGS)

## Description
The dog comes close for a hug.

## Uses
Besides the obvious opportunities it provides for close contact with your favorite canine, *hugs* may also come in handy to encourage a therapy dog to come close to patients for hugs or petting. Hugging can also teach a dog to be comfortable with physical restraint.

## Prerequisites
None.

## Training Technique
Many dogs are not very comfortable with front hugs but are naturally more tolerant of side hugs. This is because they often come in close contact with each other by touching their sides together. Some even prefer to sit facing away from the person who is hugging them to get a sort of "back hug."

Determine what type of hug your dog tolerates the best before teaching this command.

> Besides showing affection, hugging can also teach a dog to be comfortable with physical restraint.

1. Encourage your dog to come

close for a hug by calling him or holding out your arms.

2. Manipulate him into the chosen *hug* position and give the *hugs* command.

3. Reward him with hugs and petting when he sits nicely for *hugs*. With repetition, he will learn what to expect when you give the command, and he will begin to adopt the position on his own. Because dogs generally enjoy close contact with their people, this is a self-rewarding behavior that usually doesn't require any additional incentive.

## JUMP UP (ALSO: UP HERE)

### Description
The dog jumps onto whatever surface his handler indicates.

### Uses
This useful command can instruct your dog to jump into the back of an SUV or jump onto a grooming table for some well-deserved primping. Think of all the things you might want to instruct him to jump up on, including your bed, couch, chair, wagon, cart, boat, etc.

### Prerequisites
None.

### Training Technique
Be aware of your dog's physical limitations when teaching this command. Never ask him to jump any height or onto any object that may injure him. Special care must be taken with short-legged, long-backed dogs who may require pet stairs to reach higher places.

Like the *jump* command in Chapter 11, teach your dog to jump up on only one item at first. Once he has mastered that, you may teach him to jump up on other items, which will help him learn to generalize this command.

A useful command, *jump up* can instruct your dog to get into the back of an SUV or jump onto a grooming table for some well-deserved primping.

1. Most dogs enjoy car rides, and it doesn't take much to convince them to jump into the back of a vehicle, but if your dog is reluctant or apprehensive, use a food reward to lure him to do

so. Give the *jump up* command while holding the treat near the place you want him to jump.

2. When your dog jumps up, say the cue word *yes!* and reward him with the treat. Practice will condition him to eventually respond to *jump up* without food incentive. Use the same training technique to teach him to jump onto a grooming table or any other surface.

## PAWS UP

### Description
The dog puts his front paws up on a bed, table, or other item.

### Uses
*Paws up* is a handy skill for therapy dogs; they can put their paws up on beds so patients can reach them for petting. It is also helpful in getting a larger dog onto a grooming table without having to lift him entirely; just ask him to put his front paws up on the table and then lift his back end up.

> *Paws up* is a skill therapy dogs learn so they know when to put their paws on a patient's bed.

### Prerequisites
None.

### Training Technique
Your dog may not generalize this command very well, so teach him to put his paws up on the specific objects to which you want this command to apply. Therapy dogs can learn this command by practicing on a bed at home.

1. Use a treat to lure your dog into putting his front feet up on a bed or table. Keep the treat near the edge of the bed or table because you do not want to encourage him to jump onto the furniture. When he puts only his paws up, say the cue word *yes!* and then reward him.
2. When he has put his paws up successfully a few times, begin using the *paws up* command so that he can associate it with the behavior.
3. Then instead of luring him with the treat, start using your hand to pat the surface where you want him to put his feet and then give the *paws up* command. When he complies, reward him with a treat and a *yes!*.
4. When your dog performs this skill consistently, fade out the food rewards and expect him to obey without the incentive of food. Be sure to use *good* whenever he does as you ask.

## SIT UP

### Description
The dog transitions from a *down* to a *sit*.

### Uses
Teaching the *sit up* command is a good obedience exercise. When done repetitively in combination with *down*, it's called

**Sit up** can help get your dog into a sitting position for grooming, training, or veterinary exams.

"puppy pushups." In this sense, it can be a fun trick to show your friends what great shape your pup is in. It is a useful maneuver in the sport of canine musical freestyle, and it can also help get your dog into a sitting position for grooming, training, or veterinary exams.

## Prerequisites
*Sit* and *down.*

## Training Technique
If your dog knows the *down* command, he already knows how to do half the pushup by going from a *sit* to a *down*. It's then just a matter of teaching him how to go from a *down* to a *sit*.

1. Tell your dog to *sit* and then tell him to *down*.

2. Say the *sit up* command, and encourage him to rise back into a sitting position by luring his head up with a treat. If he succeeds, say the cue word *yes!*, and then reward him with the treat. If he does not, put him back into a *down* and try again. If he keeps rising into a *stand* instead of a *sit*, you may be holding the treat too far away from him. Keep it in front of his nose, and when his front end rises, draw the treat over the top of his head as if you are teaching the *sit* command.

For your dog's well-being, it's important for you to be able to handle him properly and safely. Take the time to train him to tolerate handling.

3. When your dog learns how to transition from a *down* to a *sit*, you can begin to use only your hand, rather than a treat, to encourage him to sit up. Hold your hand palm up and crossways to your dog, and lift it straight up in front of him. Eventually, you can diminish this exaggerated hand signal so that you can do a palm up signal in front of your body, which would look like the exact opposite of the hand signal for a *down*. Then you'll be able to go up and down with your hand while your dog does his pushups.

## STAND (ALSO: UP UP)

### Description
The dog stands up from a *sit* or *down*, or he stands still.

### Uses
This skill is especially valuable during grooming, but it also comes in handy during veterinary visits and show training. You can use it in a canine musical freestyle routine, to teach a standing *stay*,

The *stand* command is useful any time you need your dog to stand up or stand still, such as during veterinary visits.

or for any other time you need your dog to stand up or stand still.

### Prerequisites
*Sit*, *down*, and *stay*.

### Training Technique

You must first decide which definition you want for the *stand* command: stand up or stand still. If your dog tends to be fidgety and move around a lot during grooming or examinations, you may want to define this word as stand still, in which case you will need to use another cue word, like *up up*, to mean stand up.

If you choose to define this command as stand up, you also need to decide if you want this command to apply to both *stand up* from a *sit* and *stand up* from a *down*. (There is also the option of teaching your dog to transition from a *down* to a *sit* with the *sit up* command, which would eliminate having to teach him to stand from a *down*, as you would first tell your dog to *sit up* and then tell him to *stand* using the relevant commands.)

**Reward your dog for standing for progressively longer periods of time.**

### To Teach Stand (Up)

1. Start out with your dog in the *sit* position. Give the *stand* command, and then encourage him to stand up by putting your hand underneath his belly near his hindquarters and tickling him until he lifts his back end. You can also

encourage him to stand up by practicing on leash and gently pulling him forward one step—taking a step forward will cause him to automatically stand up.

2. When he has risen all the way into a standing position, say the cue word *yes!* and reward him immediately.

3. It helps to give your dog the *stay* command after he has reached a standing position, as you do not want him to get in the habit of sitting back down immediately after he stands. Reward him for maintaining his standing position for progressively longer periods of time.

4. Repeat Steps 1 through 3 while encouraging your dog to stand up on his own with less physical help from you. He will soon stand on his own and maintain the *stand* command for as long as you'd like.

5. To teach your dog to stand up from a *down*, make sure he has mastered the *stand* command from a *sit* first. Then repeat the same training steps with your dog starting from a *down*.

## To Teach Stand (Still)

1. If you have a particularly energetic, fidgety dog, practice Exercise First from Chapter 4 before training this skill.

2. To begin, teach your dog to stand from a *sit* (and stand from a *down*, if desired) using *up up* as the command word.

3. Teaching him to stand still is similar to teaching the *stay* command, but in addition to requiring him to maintain his place, you will require him to maintain a standing body position. While he is standing, give the *stand* command.

If he holds his position for a couple seconds, say the cue word *yes!* and reward him. If he moves even one step, move him back to his original position and start over.

4. Require your dog to maintain his standing position for successively longer periods of time before giving him a *yes!* and a reward.

5. Although food rewards can help expedite this training, your dog can learn this skill without food rewards if you consistently make him stand still for grooming. Get him into a standing position and give the *stand* command. If he moves, say the cue word *uh-uh* and move him back to his original position. Tell him *good* whenever he stands nicely. Eventually, your dog will understand what you want him to do, and he'll make like a statue when you say, "Stand."

# HOUSEHOLD MANNERS

The term "manners" carries with it an expectation of politeness and social etiquette, but its true definition is actually much broader than that. Manners include customs, habits, and a way of living. In the context of our relationship with dogs, manners are generalized for the purpose of teaching them how to live with us. It's obvious that to get the most out of our relationship with them, we need to invite them to live in our homes. Realistically, how much companionship could we enjoy with a pet who was kept outdoors in a kennel or confined to a garage or basement? There are innumerable benefits for both dogs and people when they live closely together, but this requires dogs to learn our "ways of living" so that they can fit into our homes and culture with a minimum of conflict. Remember, canines came to live with humans, not the other way around. If humans had gone to live with canines, we would have had to learn how to survive in their world.

This chapter teaches commands that make it easier for dogs to fit in to our households, as well as

Basic commands help you teach your dog good manners, which will enable him to fit into your household and become a welcome family member.

communication signals that make it easier for humans to establish and manage appropriate behaviors that will enable them to become welcome members of the family.

## DOGGIES (ALSO: PUPPIES)

### Description
This command only pertains to multiple-dog situations. All dogs in a household learn to respond to it as if it were their name.

### Uses
The *doggies* command eliminates the need to call each dog individually. It gets the attention of all dogs at once.

### Prerequisites
None.

### Training Technique
The same rules apply to the use of this command as apply to the use of your dogs' names: Keep your dogs' association with this command positive, and only use it to get their attention. It's not a replacement for the *come* command.

1. Dogs in a multi-dog household tend to learn this command quite easily when it is used regularly in phrases like "*doggies*, this way," "*doggies*, wait up," and "*doggies*, let's go to bed."
2. As pack animals, dogs are very good at functioning as a unit. However, you can heighten their responsiveness to this command by using it frequently in situations that provide desirable outcomes for them, such as in phrases

like "*doggies*, outside," "*doggies*, treats," and "*doggies*, go for a ride?"

## HEY!

### Description
This command means "Pay attention, I'm talking to you!" The dog looks at and pays attention to his handler. It is differentiated from the *look* command in Chapter 7 by the fact that you can

*Hey!* is a good command to use when you need to break your dog's attention from whatever is preoccupying him.

also use it to break your dog's focus or interrupt inappropriate behavior, in which case it means "Stop what you are doing right now!"

## Uses

*Hey!* is a good command to use when you need to break your dog's attention from whatever is preoccupying him, such as scents or things that excite his prey drive. It is more forceful and effective to get his attention than to use his name. It is especially useful when you are unable to use touch or leash communication to break his concentration.

## Prerequisites

None.

## Training Technique

The effectiveness of this command depends on never allowing your dog to ignore it. By consistently expecting him to redirect his focus when you issue a *hey!*, he will gain self-control over his natural drives. This command can be used in combination with *leave it* if you need to break your dog's focus on a particular object or animal before telling him to ignore it.

1. When your dog is intensely focused on something, like a scent trail, and won't listen to you, issue the *hey!* command firmly. Clap your hands loudly as you approach him until he stops what he's doing to pay attention to you. Initially, you may have to walk all the way up to him and take him by the collar to get him to break his focus.

2. Once you have your dog's attention,

say his name and tell him what you'd like him to do by giving commands like "Spike, *let's go*" or "Spike, *get your toy.*"

3. When your dog understands what *hey!* means, you should no longer have to approach him to get him to respond to it.

## IT'S NOTHING (ALSO: IT'S OKAY)

### Description
The dog stops barking an alert.

### Uses
Use this command to assure your dog that there is no need to be worried. When you say *it's nothing* after investigating his

## Canine Neighborhood Ambassadors

Even though the commands you and your dog will learn in this chapter focus on household living, think about the widespread impact his good manners will have on your overall life as well as his. Manners extend into his daily interactions with people in public. They extend into other domiciles—the homes of your friends and relatives, stores, parks, RVs or camper trailers, hotels, etc. They also teach and support self-control, which carries over into everything your dog does, both inside and outside your home.

barking alert, it is an indication he should stop barking. You can also use this command to help calm him when he feels nervous, such as when he is upset about the noise of fireworks or storms, or when he is fearful of a particular object.

## Prerequisites
Teach this in conjunction with *quiet*.

## Training Technique
It is easiest for your dog to learn the meaning of this word within the context of alert investigation. Then you can begin to use this command in other situations to reassure him.

1. When your dog barks an alert, go investigate.
2. If the threat is benign, issue the *it's nothing* command and calmly walk away. This acknowledges that you have evaluated the threat and determined that there's no need to be worried.
3. If your dog values your judgment as a trustworthy canine leader, he should stop barking. However, if he does keep barking, teach him the *quiet* command.
4. When your dog accepts your judgment and consistently ceases barking whenever you use the *it's nothing* command, you can begin to use it in other situations to reassure him nothing is wrong.

# KENNEL (ALSO: CRATE, DEN)

## Description
The dog goes into his crate when told to do so.

## Uses
A dog who willingly enters his crate is much easier to manage. Use this command when you crate your dog at bedtime, while in a vehicle, or when you travel. Use it when you need to give your dog a time out or to separate him from children or other animals.

## Prerequisites
None.

## Training Technique
Teaching your dog to go into his crate on command is only a part of crate training. You also want him to remain in his crate without fussing. The following training techniques cover both of these aspects. (Please see the Crate Training section in Chapter 5 for background information and rules concerning the proper use of crates.)

The crate is a tool, and, as such, you must use it judiciously. Creating a positive perception of it is fundamental to achieving desirable behaviors. The following steps will help you properly introduce your dog to his crate.

1. Keep the crate in an accessible location, with the door open so that your dog has the freedom to explore it at will. Outfit it with a comfortable pad, and keep some toys in it to make it interesting for him.
2. Help your dog become comfortable entering the crate by placing treats in or near the door. When he is comfortable retrieving the treats, start placing them farther inside the crate. You can increase his

comfort level by occasionally throwing toys into the crate for him to fetch as well.

3. When your dog progresses to the point that he will completely enter to retrieve a treat, you may begin to use the *kennel* command so that he associates it with going inside the crate.

4. Your dog must be completely comfortable entering his crate at the *kennel* command before moving on to the next step. Then you will be ready to shut the door and confine him for the first time. When you do this, make sure he has something to keep him busy in there, like a bone to chew or a food-stuffed toy. Only leave the door closed for a few minutes.

5. Gradually increase the amount of time you leave the crate door closed. Your dog may begin to express some impatience and a desire to get out, but you must be very careful at this stage because he may learn that fussing gets him an exit pass. Wait until he is quiet before releasing him.

This training may take a few weeks to complete, but your dog will eventually learn to remain quietly crated for up to several hours.

> Use the *kennel* command when you crate your dog at bedtime, while in a vehicle, or when you travel.

# LEAVE IT (ALSO: DON'T TOUCH)

## Description
The dog discontinues interest in whatever has captured his attention and leaves it alone.

## Uses
This command is commonly used to instruct a dog not to eat food that he finds on the floor, but its uses are much more far-reaching. Besides using it to get him to leave the hors d'oeuvres on the coffee table alone, use it for situations like getting him to ignore another animal, abandon a scent trail, leave the kitty litter box alone, or refrain from rolling in stinky stuff. Basically, you can use this command any time you need your dog to ignore something.

## Prerequisites
None.

## Training Technique
Because food is an item of high interest, teach your dog to ignore food first. Then you can begin to use *leave it* in other situations so that he can generalize its use.

1. You'll need a food item to use as bait. In the beginning, choose food that is not highly desirable to your dog, like a dry piece of kibble. Put it on the floor, and with

> The *leave it* command is useful any time you want your dog to ignore something that he shouldn't have or that may be harmful to him.

your dog on a leash, walk him past the item. Initially, the food should be out of his reach. If he shows interest in it, tell him *leave it* and guide him past it.

2. If your dog breaks his focus and looks at you, issue a *yes!* and reward him with a food item that is more desirable than the bait food.

3. Practice walking your dog closer to the bait food as he shows self-control and obedience in this exercise.

4. When your dog can obey the *leave it* command while walking within reach of the bait food, it's time to increase its value. Choose something that is more delectable to him, and repeat Steps 1 through 3.

5. When your dog becomes proficient in the *leave it* command in this type of scenario, you can begin to fade the use of food rewards and start using this command in other situations.

Using the *let's go to bed* command prepares your dog to go to bed and settles him down for the night.

## LET'S GO TO BED

### Description
The dog prepares to go to bed for the night.

### Uses
Nighttime routines are useful for settling

dogs down in the evening and preventing nighttime disturbances.

## Prerequisites
None.

## Training Technique
Your dog can learn this command very easily if you use it consistently and follow a prescribed pattern of activity at bedtime.

1. Issue the *let's go to bed* command, and take your dog through his normal bedtime routine, which should include a potty break.
2. If he normally sleeps on your bed, take him to your bedroom and encourage him to come onto the bed. If he normally sleeps in a crate, take him to it and bed him down. If he normally sleeps on a dog bed, take him to his bed and ask him to lie down.

Eventually, your dog will understand what these words mean and perform his bedtime routine without guidance from you.

## MOVE (ALSO: LOOK OUT, EXCUSE ME)

## Description
The dog moves out of the way.

## Uses
Move asks your dog to move out of the way when he's blocking a doorway, lying in your path, or occupying a spot on the couch where you want to sit. It is especially useful when you're carrying groceries into the house, moving furniture, or any time your hands are full and you cannot physically make him move. Also, it

## End on a Positive Note
Obedience commands are a great way for you to assert your authority and give your dog an opportunity to appease you. Your final praise will conclude any inappropriate behavioral incidents in a positive way, which will encourage his continued trust, respect, and obedience.

can help teach him to give way to young children, which helps prevent conflicts.

## Prerequisites
None.

## Training Technique
Always issue this command in a firm tone of voice.

1. To teach your dog to move on demand, simply give the *move* command in a firm voice and physically crowd him out of the way. You can also take him by the collar and lead him out of the way until he begins to understand what you want. If you expect him to relinquish his place on the couch or bed, make it easy for him to do the right thing by providing an alternative place for him to repose, such as a dog bed on the floor.
2. To teach your dog to yield to children (rather than stand their ground), firmly issue the *move* command whenever a child comes near him, and lead him by the collar, if necessary, to make him get up and move. He will soon learn

that children, too, have the right-of-way. It is a good safety measure to teach him to retreat like this when he is the target of unwanted attention from children, but never allow them to relentlessly pester your dog. Provide him with a peaceful haven away from children if the situation requires intervention, and use door gates or other barriers to separate him from children when you cannot supervise them.

# NAUGHTY (ALSO: NAUGHTY DOG, BAD DOG)

## Description
This lets your dog know you are displeased with something he's done.

## Uses
Just as you need to let your dog know when he does something that pleases you, you also need to let him know when he displeases you. This command is

## Right-of-Way

A dog who yields and gives his owner the right-of-way is behaving respectfully. To achieve and maintain this kind of status, it is a good policy to reserve furniture for people first and dogs second. There is absolutely no reason to feel guilty for making your dog move when a human wants to occupy his place on the couch!

typically used after the *uh-uh* or *hey!* commands, which are intended to stop an undesired behavior. *Naughty* is also a power command that helps to nurture your dog's will to please, as he will seek to avoid doing things that result in this reprimand.

## Prerequisites
None.

## Training Technique
Your dog will understand this command simply from the tone of your voice.

1. Always issue the *naughty* command in a low, disgusted tone of voice. You do not need to repeat it more than a few times or carry on with it for an extended period, as it will begin to lose its effect with overuse. Dogs who are extremely loyal may be exceptionally sensitive to it, in which case you should use it sparingly and only for the worst transgressions.

2. Be aware that if you wait too long after your dog's undesirable behavior to issue this command, he may not understand what he has done to displease you. It is best to use it immediately after stopping an undesirable behavior. It does little good to admonish him for past crimes that he has already forgotten.

3. After admonishing your dog, you can redirect him to an appropriate replacement behavior, or if there isn't a suitable alternative, require him to perform one or more obedience commands so that you can praise him with *good*.

# OFF (ALSO: GET OFF)

## Description

This command can have multiple meanings, including "don't jump on me," "get off the furniture," and "get off my lap," among many others. In general, it means "remove your paws."

## Uses

This is a good command to teach a dog who has a jumping problem or difficulty with personal space boundaries (pushy dogs). It is also a good power command because it controls movement and can help reinforce personal space. If you want your dog to vacate furniture so that you can use it yourself, use the *move* command instead.

## Prerequisites

*Sit* (in some cases) and *get your toy* (in some cases).

> Be consistent in enforcing the no jumping rule in all situations.

## Training Technique

Before teaching this command, decide which meaning you want it to have so that you can be consistent in using it for those purposes. When using this command to instruct your dog not to jump on you, make sure you are consistent in enforcing a no jumping rule in all situations, including during play.

There are several techniques you can use to discourage your dog from jumping. With any of these options, always remember to issue a *good* when your dog behaves appropriately.

1. **Withhold attention:** Firmly give the *off* command whenever your dog tries to jump on you, then turn your back to him and refuse to give him any attention until he keeps his paws off you. If he jumps on you during play, give him a time-out, and refuse to play for a few seconds until he calms down and keeps his paws off you. He will learn that he won't get any attention from you if he jumps up.

2. **Use a blocker:** Some people find success using a physical object like a board or trash can lid to block their dogs from jumping on them. Tell your dog *off*, and wait for him to stop trying to jump on you before you give him any attention. You can also use your hand as a blocker by holding your palm in front of your dog's face—when you stop his head from moving forward, you also stop his feet from moving forward.

3. **Teach a substitute behavior:** Dogs can't jump if they're busy doing something else. Teach your dog *sit* (from Chapter 7) for greetings. For this technique, use food rewards to encourage compliance. If your dog is too excited during greetings to sit down, teach him the *get your toy* command (from Chapter 11), and help him expend his energy by playing with him for a few minutes whenever you greet him.

For other situations in which you want your dog to remove his paws, use these techniques.

1. **Off the furniture:** Tell your dog *off*, and lead him off the furniture by his collar. With consistent and frequent use of this command, he will learn what it means and will begin to vacate the furniture whenever you issue it.

2. **Enforcing personal boundaries:** If your dog is particularly pushy, you'll need to adopt some strict rules concerning your personal space. Do not allow him to touch you unless you have invited him to do so. When he engages in unauthorized touching, tell him *off* firmly and push him away. Be strict about enforcing your personal space. If necessary, withhold your attention for a short time out as a consequence for inappropriate behavior.

## OUT

### Description
This command gets the dog out of a forbidden area.

### Uses
The *out* command actually has applications for indoor and outdoor situations. Use it to teach your dog which indoor areas are off limits to him, such as sensitive or dangerous areas or places where hazardous chemicals or breakable items are stored. Use it to teach him yard boundaries, such as to keep him away from shrubs, plantings, or gardens.

### Prerequisites
None.

### Training Technique
Think about what areas should be off limits to your dog so that you can consistently enforce boundary rules from the very beginning.

1. Carry some treats with you, and walk into a forbidden area. When your dog follows you, say *out* firmly, and walk toward him to shoo him out of the area.
2. When your dog retreats to his boundary line, say *yes!* and reward him.
3. Keep repeating this exercise until your dog learns to respect his boundary and no longer follows you into the forbidden area. You can further proof him by putting a leash on him and throwing a toy or treat into the forbidden area. Use the leash to prevent him from entering it. If he does not attempt to pursue the item, say *yes!* and reward him with a treat.
4. Once your dog knows what this command means, fade the food rewards and expect him to obey without them. You can then use this command in many situations, as dogs tend to generalize it quite easily.

The *out* command teaches your dog which areas are off limits to him, like your flower garden.

## OUTSIDE

### Description
The dog goes to the door so that his owner can let him go outside.

### Uses
This command is a good way to announce a potty break to your dog.

When asked as a question, it can help you determine if he needs to do his business because he will respond to it excitedly. It is also useful to get him outside quickly if he is sick and vomiting.

### Prerequisites
None.

### Training Technique
This command doesn't require any special training techniques. You only need to get into the habit of saying this command before you let your dog outside. Since dogs generally enjoy the outdoors, they tend to pick this command up quite quickly and will immediately rush to the door when they hear it.

## PLACE (ALSO: BED)

### Description
The dog goes to his designated place and lies down, usually on a rug, mat, or bed.

### Uses
This command has many convenient uses. It can help teach your dog not to beg by sending him to his designated area during your mealtimes. It can get him to settle down at bedtime. You can send him to his area if he tends to

*Place* instructs your dog to go to a designated area, which ensures he always has a spot you can send him whenever you want him to stay put, such as during mealtimes.

pester your guests. If you and your dog participate in activities away from home, a portable mat or bed will ensure he always has a spot you can send him whenever you want him to stay in one location.

### Prerequisites
*Sit*, *down*, and *stay*.

### Training Technique
You can use a rug, towel, blanket, dog bed, crate pad, rubber mat, or a similar item to designate a place marker for your dog, but always use the same item. If you want to designate more than one place for him, use a different name for each, such as bed, mat, or blanket, so that he can distinguish between them.

1. With your dog on a leash, lead him onto his place marker and issue the *place* command. Then ask him to sit or lie down. As soon as he complies, issue a *yes!* and reward him.
2. Tell your dog to do a *stay* and wait a few seconds before releasing him with an *okay*.
3. Practice Steps 1 and 2, asking your dog to stay for successively longer periods of time. Give him a treat occasionally during his *stay* to reward him for maintaining his place.
4. When your dog is consistent with Steps 1 through 3, encourage him to go to the marker on his own without leading him there. Give the *place* command, and if he complies, issue a *yes!* and reward him.
5. Practice the *place* command until your dog consistently goes to the marker on his own. You can further proof him by moving it to different

## Anybody There?

If you pay attention to your dog's barking, you'll quickly learn to recognize when he *thinks* he hears something and when he really does hear or see something. Always listen to what he is trying to tell you with his vocalizations. When his barking means something to you, he will take it more seriously, too.

locations so that he can learn to go to his place no matter where it is. This is especially helpful if you plan to use a marker while traveling or competing in dog sports.

## QUIET (ALSO: SHUSH)

### Description
The dog stops barking or whining.

### Uses
This command is particularly useful for getting vocal canines to control their barking, but it can help turn any dog into a disciplined watchdog. Use it to teach your dog how to distinguish between nonthreatening and threatening situations that warrant a barking alarm. It also can be used to discourage him from being overly reactive to other dogs, squirrels in the yard, or the neighbor's cat.

### Prerequisites
None.

## Training Technique

Always use good judgment in issuing this command in order to achieve success. For example, you cannot expect your dog to cease barking when a stimulus is increasing in intensity. If someone is approaching your door, wait until the person has stopped progressing before you ask him to be quiet. Repeating the *quiet* command when he finds it difficult or impossible to stop barking will only serve to make him unresponsive to it.

1. Initially, when your dog barks at something, always get up to investigate. If he has a good reason for barking, such as a person coming to the door or an animal encroaching on your property, praise and pet him for doing a good job.
2. If the stimulus is a benign threat, reassure your dog with *it's nothing*. If he continues to bark, issue a *quiet*. It is very important at this point to insist he be quiet because he needs to trust and acquiesce to your judgment in this matter. If he does not, move him to a place where the stimulus is not so arousing and repeat the *quiet* command. When he complies, issue a *good*.
3. If your dog barks at nothing or tends to overreact by barking at the sound of planes or people who are a block away, investigate his barking and then act extremely disappointed in his performance as a watchdog. Tell him *quiet*.
4. Eventually, your dog will learn that he has a very important job to do. When he understands the *quiet* command in this context, he'll be able to understand it in other situations as well.

# RIDE (ALSO: GO FOR A RIDE)

## Description

This command doesn't really tell the dog to do anything, but it is a good communication signal to get him to prepare to go somewhere in a vehicle.

## Uses

The purpose of *ride* is to communicate with your dog so that he knows what to expect. It is also a fun word you can use to get him in an excited, happy mood—but only if you follow through on it.

## Prerequisites

None.

## Training Technique

Since dogs generally love to go places in a vehicle, you only need to say this command consistently a few times for your dog to grasp its meaning.

1. If you like to use this word to generate excitement in your dog, say it enthusiastically as a question.
2. If you want to use it to prepare your dog to get in the car, say it as a statement.

# TREAT (ALSO: COOKIE, GOODIE)

## Description

The dog immediately focuses on his handler to get a treat.

## Uses

This command is fun to use if you want to get your dog excited, but it is especially useful in emergency

situations. If he has gotten loose and has not yet learned *come* reliably, *treat* may convince him to come back to you. If your dog doesn't have the self-control to stop chasing a wild animal or gets into a potentially dangerous situation, *treat* may provide a way to distract him and redirect his attention.

## Prerequisites
None.

## Training Technique
Teaching your dog to recognize the *treat* command simply entails using it every time you give him a special treat. Say it with excitement to give it more value.

1. Because you want your dog to respond to this command in any situation, offer treats at different times and in different locations—don't offer them at the same time and place every day, and don't make treats a part of your routine. Keep treat-giving spontaneous so that your dog knows they may come at any time and in any place. This is one case when spoiling your dog has a definite purpose.

> Dogs generally love to go places in a vehicle, so you only need to say the *ride* command consistently a few times for your dog to grasp its meaning.

2. There is just one warning to heed in the use of this command: Do not become too reliant on *treat* to control your dog. It can easily become a crutch and an excuse to neglect teaching your dog

very important commands like *come* and *leave it*. It can also become your dog's name with overuse, so take the time to teach him to respond to his name and obedience commands with just as much enthusiasm as he responds to *treat*.

## UP (ALSO: COME UP)

### Description
The dog jumps up onto whatever the handler designates.

### Uses
This command serves as an invitation for your dog to join you. It gives him permission to invade your space, whether that space is on the bed, the couch, or on your lap.

### Prerequisites
None.

### Training Technique
A dog who waits for an invitation to invade his owner's space is acting respectfully.

1. Make a habit of telling your dog *up* just before he jumps onto your bed or couch to be near you. This lets him know that he enjoys such close contact with you only because you allow it, not because he takes it.
2. When you'd like to enjoy some cuddle time with your dog, it shouldn't take much more than a pat on the furniture or your lap and an encouraging *up* to convince him to join you. Once he learns the meaning of this command

through consistent use, you can eventually eliminate having to pat anything and just use the command.

## WAIT

### Description
The dog holds a position or pauses for a short duration.

### Uses
The *wait* command is an extremely useful power command that all dogs should learn. You can use it to keep your dog from rushing out the door when people are coming and going, and it can also help rehabilitate a dog who has a habit of rushing out the door and running away. You can make your dog wait before jumping out of a vehicle so that you'll have time to get his leash on, and you can make him wait at doorways so that he doesn't push, crowd, or trip people who are already coming through the door. Use this command any time you need him to pause for a moment.

### Prerequisites
None.

### Training Technique
*Wait* is different from *stay* because it only requires your dog to hold his position for a very brief length of time. If you want him to hold his position longer than a few seconds, teach him the *stay* command in Chapter 7. *Wait* most often applies to going through doors, such as when entering or exiting a building or vehicle.

This particular skill does not necessarily require the use of food rewards, though they do tend to expedite the learning process. If you prefer to train without food, replace *yes!* with *good*, and replace the food rewards with petting and praise.

1. With your dog on leash at your side, stand by a door and give him the *wait* command. You may want to use the hand signal for *stay* (palm facing your dog).

2. Open the door just a crack and be prepared to block your dog with your leg if he tries to rush through it. If he maintains his position, issue a *yes!* and reward him. If he tries to go through the door, say *uh-uh* and pull him back to your side to start over.

3. When your dog will maintain a *wait* with the door cracked open a little bit, try opening it a little more each time you practice this exercise. Always be prepared to prevent him from going through the door by using your leg or body to block him.

4. If your dog will maintain his *wait* even when the door is wide open,

> *Wait* is different from *stay* because it only requires your dog to hold his position for a very brief length of time. For example, you can use it to keep him from rushing out the door.

it's time to give him an *okay* and let him pass through it. You can now practice making him wait and then telling him *okay* whenever you want him to go through a door.

5. When your dog has mastered this skill on leash, try practicing it off leash as well. Reinforce it by requiring him to wait every time he goes through a door, including at the vet's office or when getting in or out of the car. People will be amazed at his good manners! You can also use this command in other situations where you would like him to stay still for just a few seconds.

## WHAT'S THAT?

### Description
The dog checks to see what's going on and determines whether or not he should bark.

### Uses
This command can help hone your dog's watchdog skills by teaching him to be alert to sounds. It is also a way to activate your canine alarm system at will—it can signify to him that a property or perimeter check is required.

### Prerequisites
None.

### Training Technique
The purpose of *what's that?* is not to get your dog to bark; it's to get him to check for any threats. If he barks first and checks later, he's not doing his job correctly. Say *uh-uh* if he barks

inappropriately, and teach him the *quiet* command, if necessary, so that he can learn how to distinguish between appropriate and inappropriate barking.

The *what's that?* command can help hone your dog's watchdog skills by teaching him to be alert.

1. Teaching your dog *what's that?* basically entails showing him what to do. When you hear a sound, issue a *what's that?* and get up to investigate it yourself.

2. Most dogs will automatically jump up to investigate with their owners, but if yours doesn't, encourage him to get up and investigate with you. If you want to teach your dog to check the view from certain windows, investigate the same windows in the same order each time, usually starting with the window that offers the greatest vantage point.

This will help teach him how to do a thorough investigation.

3. Discourage barking unless there is, indeed, something to bark at. Issue a *good* when he alerts you to appropriate things.
4. Eventually, you will be able to say *what's that?*, and your dog will investigate for you.

## WHO'S HERE?

### Description
The dog gets excited and prepares to greet someone who is arriving.

### Uses
Some people love to be greeted by a wagging tail, and *who's here?* can help you get your dog in the mood to give an enthusiastic greeting to a family member or guest. Unlike *what's that?*, barking is permitted or even encouraged with the *who's here?* command because it gives these words another potential use as an emergency alert. If you feel scared or threatened, or think there may be a burglar in your house, issue a *who's here?* to get your dog barking.

### Prerequisites
None.

### Training Technique
*Who's here?* is only appropriate for dogs who can greet people nicely. If your dog gets overly excited and jumps up on them, you do not want to excite him even further by using this command. Also, dogs who tend to crowd or rush the door may be better off learning *back off* from Chapter 10 rather than *who's here?* If your dog is a good candidate to learn *who's here?* and you genuinely enjoy seeing how happy he is to greet people, you may also want to teach him *quiet* (in this chapter) or *easy* (from Chapter 8) so that you can tell him when it's time to calm down.

1. When people are arriving, give the *who's here?* command in a very excited voice, and encourage your dog to go see who's coming to the door.
2. Act excited and happy when people enter our home, and your dog will do the same.

*Who's here?* gets your dog excited and prepared to greet someone who is arriving.

# 10

# OUT AND ABOUT

**J**ust because dogs make great house pets does not mean they should be kept indoors all the time! One of the characteristics they share with humans is their sociability, and you will be missing out on many excellent adventures with your dog if you do not take him out and about once in a while. Do you enjoy walking or jogging? Why not do it with your dog? Do you enjoy camping, boating, and other outdoor activities? Why not include your dog? Do you like traveling? Why not take your dog with you?

There are also a great many canine sports and activities in which your dog may love to participate or compete, but there are a few things to consider before you take him out in public. You need to be concerned about how your dog will react to other animals he will encounter, how he'll behave around people, including children, and how much control you'll have over him, especially if you want to enjoy off-leash activities.

This chapter offers many wonderful commands that address these

> You'll miss out on many fun adventures with your dog if you don't take him out and about once in a while.

concerns and make it a pleasure to include your dog in your life away from home. As a bonus, commands make it easier to control him so that you can greatly increase his safety. For example, they can help prevent him from running into the street, getting into a fight with another animal, or getting lost. Likewise, they can also keep others safe because a controlled pet does not run at large to cause accidents or bite people. And perhaps the greatest benefit of all is that a well-behaved dog out on the town gives the public a positive perception of our canine companions. When you take your dog out and about, remember that he is an ambassador for dogs and owners everywhere.

## BACK (ALSO: BACK UP, REVERSE)

### Description
The dog moves backward on command.

### Uses
This command can get your dog out of the way or out of a tight spot. It is also valuable in any sport that requires control of the dog's movement, such as canine musical freestyle or herding.

### Prerequisites
None.

### Training Technique
It's fairly easy to encourage a dog to move backward simply by walking toward him and crowding him to pressure him to back up. The hard part, however, is to get him to back up in a straight line.

## Reverse Treat-Steering Method

1. Encourage your dog to move straight back by holding treats in both of your hands and holding them out to each side of his head. When you move close to him to pressure him to back up, tease him with each treat alternately in an attempt to steer him in a straight line as he's backing up.

2. If your dog takes a couple of straight backward steps, tell him *yes!* and reward him immediately.

3. Gradually increase the number of backward steps your dog must take before you reward him. When he can back up a short distance, start using the *back* command when you want him to back up. He will then learn to associate the command with this new skill.

4. When your dog successfully backs in a straight line, stop crowding him and try to get him to perform *back* at your command alone. A good hand signal to use for this skill is a pushing motion.

## Channel Method

1. If your dog does not respond well to reverse treat steering, try barriers to encourage him to back up in a straight line. Construct a channel using long barriers on both sides, such as walls, couches, rows of chairs, or fencing to keep him on the right course while backing up. With your dog within the channel, crowd him to encourage him to back up.

2. If he takes a few steps backward, issue a *yes!* and reward him immediately.

3. Gradually increase the number of steps your dog must take before you reward him. When he can back up a short distance, start using the *back* command when you want him to back up.

4. Then practice this skill using a barrier on only one side. When your dog can back up straight with only one barrier, you can attempt to eliminate the barriers altogether and practice in the open.

5. When your dog successfully backs up in a straight line, stop crowding him and try to get him to perform *back* at your command alone. A good hand signal to use for this skill is a pushing motion.

# BACK OFF

## Description

This command instructs the dog to create and maintain a distance between himself and a human or an animal.

## Uses

*Back off* is based on herding commands, but it has several practical uses for pet dogs. In the case of dogs who tend to crowd the doorway when guests attempt to enter, *back off* is a more concise way of saying, "Back away from the door." Combined with the

> The *back* command can get your dog out of the way or out of a tight spot.

*wait* command, you can instruct your dog to hold off on greeting guests until they have entered the house and you have given him permission to meet them. It can help keep him from getting too aroused during exuberant introductions. *Back off* can also help prevent fights with other dogs or wild animals, and it may even prevent a nasty encounter with a skunk! You can also use this command to discourage your dog from harassing the cat. These are power commands because they allow you to greet people at the door first, and they put you in a position of control regarding your dog's encounters with animals and people.

### Prerequisites
*Wait.*

### Training Technique
Whether you use this command to teach your dog to greet visitors more civilly or to back off an animal that does not appreciate his advances, the training technique is basically the same: Use your body to crowd him away from the human or animal that has captured his interest.

The *back off* command instructs the dog to create and maintain a distance between himself and a human or an animal.

### Guests
Dogs who respect their owners (especially their owners' personal space) will relinquish territory to their owners quite readily and learn to back off. With

consistent practice, your dog will soon learn to allow people through your door without rushing at them or crowding the doorway.

1. When someone comes to visit, open the door wide enough for one person to pass through it and ask your guest to wait until you give her permission to enter. If your dog is like most dogs, he'll be clamoring impatiently for a chance to get a sniff of the person at the door.

2. Block the doorway with your body, and give the *back off* command. Pressure him to back up by moving toward him and crowding him away from the door, pushing him gently with your legs, if necessary.

3. Then give the *wait* command. When he complies, allow your guest to enter. When your guest has comfortably entered the home, release your dog with an *okay* to give your guest a greeting. As long as he is proficient in *wait*, you should not need to keep him on a leash to prevent him from rushing at your guest. Require him to go through the *back off/wait* routine for every guest, not just particular ones. This way, it will become a normal greeting procedure for him.

4. When your dog performs *back off* at your verbal command (without physical pressure from you), begin to open the door wider and allow visitors to enter more normally. Of course, don't forget to give him a well-deserved *good* each time he waits for an *okay* cue to greet visitors!

## Cats

If there is a chance your dog may engage in pet cat harassment or come into contact with a potentially dangerous wild animal or aggressive dog, it is best to teach him *back off* in a less volatile setting initially.

1. With your dog and cat separated by a door gate, wait until he is showing interest in the cat and then wedge your body between him and the gate. Teach him to move away from it by telling him *back off* and crowding him away from it.

2. When your dog responds to *back off*, try to back him off the cat while he is on a leash. Allow him to show interest in the cat, and then tell him to *back off* and pressure him to comply. Always remember to give him a *good* when he responds appropriately.

3. When your dog appears to respond consistently to the *back off* command while on a leash, you can try it off leash.

## Other Animals

*Back off* is a good skill to practice when meeting strange dogs while out for walks.

1. Allow your dog to greet another dog for a few seconds, and then tell him *back off*. Make him move away by getting your body between both dogs and crowding your dog to make him back up. (Note: Never attempt to get between your dog and another animal if they are engaged in a physical confrontation!)

2. Tell your dog *good* each time he responds appropriately. Eventually, he

will perform *back off* at your command without physical pressure.

# BE CLOSE (ALSO: BY ME)

## Description
The dog comes closer to his handler without performing a full *come*.

## Uses
This command is a good safety measure to use when your dog is off leash and unfamiliar people or animals are approaching, or any time you need to keep a close eye on him when he's off leash. Because *be close* controls your dog's movement, this is an effective power command.

## Prerequisite
*Come.*

## Training Technique
Any off-leash dog should respond reliably to the *come* command. However, do not use the *come* command to teach this skill because you should only use it if you want your dog to come within reach.

1. To encourage your dog to come closer to you, issue a be close and clap your hands, slap your thighs, squat down, or whistle to coax him closer.
2. When your dog comes within 5 to 10 feet (1.5 to 3 m) of you, tell him *good* so that he knows he's close enough. If you are consistent in the amount of distance you require in this exercise,

> The *be close* command is a good safety measure to use when your dog is off leash and unfamiliar people or animals are approaching, or any time you need to keep a close eye on him when he's off leash.

and you practice *be close* frequently, he will soon have a clear idea of what you expect of him.

# BEHIND ME (ALSO: FOLLOW)

## Description
The dog walks directly behind his handler.

## Uses
This is a useful position when walking on a narrow path, when the handler needs to separate his dog from a potentially dangerous situation ahead, or any other time is it advantageous to have a dog following behind. It is a useful skill in the sport of canine musical freestyle or for those who enjoy hiking with their dogs. Since *behind me* helps provide movement control and also puts the handler in a first position, this is a useful power command.

## Prerequisites
None.

## Training Technique
If you are already using the *by me* command, choose the alternative command *follow* for this skill, as your dog may not be able to distinguish between *by me* and *behind me*.

1. This skill is easiest to teach by holding a treat behind your back and using it to

> *Behind me* is used any time is it advantageous to have a dog following behind you or to keep him from a potentially dangerous situation ahead.

encourage your dog to follow behind you. Tell him *behind me*, and hold the treat as low as possible to prevent him from jumping up to get it. Walk a few steps, and if he follows, issue a *yes!* and reward him with the treat.

2. When your dog will consistently follow you for a few steps, begin to increase the distance you expect him to follow before giving him a *yes!* and reward.

3. You can also begin to point behind your back instead of holding a treat there when giving the *behind me* command. This will become your hand signal when you want your dog to get behind you. Continue to give him a *yes!* and reward when he does as you wish.

4. When your dog has a clear understanding of what you expect when you issue a *behind me*, it is time to try this skill while out and about with him. Give him the command and hand signal for *behind me*, and if he complies, tell him *good*. If he is reluctant to comply without a food reward, practice with him on leash and encourage him to obey by holding the leash behind your back. He will quickly understand that you expect compliance, even in the absence of food rewards.

# GEE (ALSO: TURN RIGHT)

## Description
The dog turns right.

## Uses
*Gee* (pronounced jee) is the partner command to *haw* (which instructs a dog to turn left). Both commands come from the sport of dog sledding, and both are power commands in the sense that they control the dog's movement. The *gee* command is useful any time a dog is in harness for pulling (sledding or carting). It also allows a handler to prepare her dog to make a change in direction, whether he is on or off leash. Canine musical freestylers sometimes use this command to instruct their dogs to perform a right side-pass (walk sideways to the right), but this is an entirely different skill that is not covered in this definition.

## Prerequisites
None.

## Training Technique
The easiest way to teach your dog directional cues is to use them frequently while walking him on a leash in the *heel* position.

1. Teach *gee* and *haw* (also in this chapter) at the same time, issuing these commands a second before making a direction change. Your dog will begin to anticipate the turns. Be sure to make full 90-degree turns so that it's obvious to him what the commands mean.

2. When you notice your dog anticipating the turns, start using the commands when he is walking ahead of you, either on leash or in harness. He may look back at you for reassurance that he's going the correct way. You can help him through this transition period by pointing with your finger in the direction you want to go. When he

gains confidence, he'll begin making the turns without looking back.

## GET BACK (ALSO: SEAT, FLOOR)

### Description
This command instructs a dog to move to the back of a vehicle or to a specific seat or area in a vehicle.

### Uses
In the interest of keeping dogs safe and keeping their hair off the seats, it is always a good idea to have a designated area in your vehicle for your dog to stay put in during the ride. This area may be a particular seat with a doggy seatbelt, an area on the floor, or a cargo area in the back of a van or SUV. You may apply this command to almost any type of conveyance, including an automobile, boat, or RV.

### Prerequisites
*Stay, sit*, and *down.*

### Training Technique
The intention of this command is to instruct your dog to go to a specific place in your vehicle—it does not tell him what to do when he gets there. Your dog needs to be well versed in the *stay* command (see Chapter 7) if you want him to remain in his place. In addition, if you prefer him to remain lying down or sitting while traveling, you will have to teach *sit* or *down* separately (see Chapter 7) and insist that he maintain the desired position whenever the vehicle is in motion.

1. When your dog enters your vehicle, usher him to his special spot by leading him there by the collar or shooing him to the back of the vehicle. Give the *get back* command while doing this. When he gets there, tell him *good* and *stay.* Food rewards are not necessary for this particular skill.

2. Teaching *get back* is simply a matter of establishing good habits. When you consistently urge your dog to take his proper place in the vehicle whenever he travels with you, he will eventually take his position automatically when you issue the *get back* command. If he does not want to take his place, refuse to go anywhere until he does. Most dogs love vehicle rides so much they quickly learn to obey their owner's wishes so that they can get on with it.

## GO HOME

### Description
When out for a walk, the dog will return to his home when released to do so.

### Uses
Releasing your dog to go home can be a great way for him to expend any residual energy he may have at the end of a walk—and dogs love to run ahead of their owners. It can also function as an emergency procedure if anything should happen to you while you are out walking; your dog may very well be able to go home and fetch help for you.

### Prerequisites
*Come.*

## Training Technique

As with any off-leash skill, your dog should respond reliably to the *come* command (in Chapter 7) before you teach him *go home*. In addition, always keep safety in mind when teaching him to go home on his own. Exercise this skill only in situations where you can observe him to make sure he makes it home safely (unless you are in an emergency situation), and do not teach him to cross roads or other dangerous hazards. The *go home* command is meant to be a fun conclusion to an enjoyable walk, not an adventure in cross-country survival!

1. Your dog will quickly grasp the meaning of *go home* if you release him 5 to 10 feet (1.5 to 3 m) from your front door and encourage him to run to it ahead of you.

2. Give the *go home* command when you release him. Most dogs are anxious for a drink of water after a walk, and so it will be natural for your dog to make a beeline for the door. In the beginning stages of training, it helps to make sure there are no tempting distractions around when you release him. Squirrels, cats, dogs, or children at play may entice him to deviate from his course.

If you use the *go home* command when you are out walking your dog, he will return home when released to do so.

3. If your dog is prone to easily abandon his intended destination, encourage your wayfarer to stay on course by providing him with a treat each time he makes it to the door successfully. He will probably have a good idea of what *go home* means after just a few walks. Then you can begin to increase the distance from your front door. There is no limit to the distance you can work up to, but it is important to keep him in sight at all times and to prevent him from encountering dangerous situations on his way home.

## GO ON (ALSO: MOVE ON, MOVE ALONG, GET GOING, MUSH)

### Description
This command instructs the dog to move on from a stop.

### Uses
*Go on* is useful any time a dog has stopped and must be encouraged to move on. It is a standard command in canine sports like carting, sledding, and skijoring, but it also comes in handy during walks, both on and off leash, to let your dog know when to resume forward motion. The *go on* command is especially useful in situations that require a lot of stops and starts, such as when making deliveries or picking up trash along a road. As a form of movement control, this command joins the ranks of other power commands.

### Prerequisites
None.

## Keep Moving!

For dogs who like to stop and sniff, or males who like to stop at any vertical object to leave their calling card, use the *walk on* command instead of the *go on* command, which will prevent the dog from stopping in the first place.

### Training Technique
This command is a driving command, which means it is usually issued and enforced from behind the dog, but this is not an absolute requirement. The important thing is to be consistent in the situations for which you use it. You may want to also teach your dog *whoa* or *stop* (in this chapter) to control both stopping and starting movements.

1. Issue the *go on* command, and then encourage your dog to move forward with verbal pressure from behind. A gentle tap from behind will often get a dog to move forward. Clapping your hands may also encourage him to move.

2. Repetition will help your dog understand *go on*, but you need to insist he comply with this command every time you issue it. Dogs who have a natural drive to run, like Siberian Huskies, will pick up on this command quickly and obey it with enthusiasm, while dogs with less drive, or those prone to stop and sniff, may require more prodding.

# GO POTTY (ALSO: GET BUSY, GO POOPS)

## Description
This command instructs the dog when and where to do his business.

## Uses
Having a dog who eliminates on command is useful in many different situations, including those times when you want to make sure he has had a potty break before you leave the house, when you want to instruct him to use a designated area at home or while traveling, and when you are simply in a hurry and want him to get down to business. It also lets the dog know that he's not outside to play, and it keeps him focused on the task you want him to do.

## Prerequisites
None.

## Training Technique
You can teach your dog *go potty* either during the housetraining process or after he is already housetrained. You can also use different commands to distinguish between the two types of elimination, such as *go potty* and *go poops*; this is helpful for occasions when you want to make sure he does both.

1. Take your dog outside to a designated potty area at regular times during the day, especially when he is most likely to have to go, such as after eating, sleeping, or playing. This

*Go potty* instructs your dog when and where to do his business.

sets him up to obey the *go potty* command with little effort—and little prodding from you.

2. Wait until your dog begins to sniff for a spot to go, and then tell him *go potty*. When he finishes eliminating, give him plenty of praise. A food reward will give him even more incentive to go potty the next time you ask.

3. When your dog appears to do quite well when you are setting him up to succeed, begin to challenge him by asking him to potty before he starts sniffing for a spot to go. Then you can graduate to asking him to potty at times when his need to go isn't dire. Observe him at this point because he may give you a sign that he doesn't really need to go. If you know it's been a while since he has eliminated, it pays to be persistent and insist that he go anyway. When you become familiar with his elimination habits, you will get a feel for when you should persist and when you should listen to him. If he keeps putting his nose to the ground when you tell him *go potty* but he just can't seem to go, it's time to end the potty break.

4. It can be challenging to convince a dog to eliminate in an unfamiliar place when traveling. The *go potty* command is a great way to tell your dog where he can go when he is in a new environment. To make sure he doesn't associate this command only with his usual designated potty area, practice using it in other places while he is on a leash. Ask him to go potty in an appropriate area outside your veterinarian's office, at the dog park, or other suitable places. It will then become easy to use this command whenever and wherever you need it.

## Elimination Habits

If you plan to use the separate commands *go potty* and *go poops*, keep in mind that dogs urinate much more frequently and urgently than they defecate, so always ask your dog to go potty first. Because it often takes dogs longer to work up a bowel movement, give your dog plenty of time to accomplish this task. Again, it helps to observe your individual dog's elimination habits in order to learn what you can expect of him.

# GO THERE

### Description
This command instructs the dog to go to wherever his handler points.

### Uses
*Go there* is particularly useful for managing and keeping control of more than one dog or for instructing your dog exactly where you want him to be. For example, you can tell him where you want him to go inside your home, vehicle, tent, camper, or RV. You can get him out of the way when moving furnishings or carrying groceries into

the house. You can instruct him where you want him to pose for a family portrait. The uses are endless.

### Prerequisites
*Sit.*

### Training Technique
The *go there* command should indicate a spot fairly close to the handler so that the dog does not have difficulty determining where he needs to go. (This is not a good command to use if you want to instruct your dog to go across a room or across a field.) In cases where you instruct him to go to a particular place frequently, it may be more appropriate to use specific place commands, such as *bed*, *get back*, or *kennel*.

The easiest way to teach your dog *go there* is to use a treat to lure him to the place where you want him to go.

**The *go there* command instructs your dog to go exactly where you want him to be. For example, you can tell him where you want him to go inside your home or car.**

1. Begin with your dog sitting in front of you. Lure him to a position just a couple of feet (m) from his original spot with a treat. Issue the *go there* command while doing so.

2. Give the *sit* command when he reaches the new spot. When he complies, issue a *yes!* and give him the treat. Repeat these steps until your dog understands that you want him

to move from point A to point B when you issue a *go there*.

3. Then you can begin to point your finger to where you want your dog to go instead of luring him with a treat. Continue to let him know when he's done the right thing by issuing a *yes!* and rewarding him with a treat. When he responds to *go there* consistently, you can begin to fade the food rewards for this behavior.

4. Use this command in convenient situations and enforce compliance, if necessary, by crowding your dog with your body until he moves. Be sure to use *good* as a praise command after you have phased out food rewards.

# HAW (ALSO: TURN LEFT)

## Description
This command instructs a dog to turn left.

## Uses
*Haw* is the partner command to *gee* (pronounced jee), which instructs a dog to turn right. Both commands come from the sport of dog sledding and fall into the category of power commands. *Haw* is useful any time a dog is in harness for pulling, such as in dog sledding or carting. It can also serve to prepare a dog to make a change in direction, whether he is on or off leash. Canine musical freestylers sometimes use this command to instruct their dogs to perform a left side-pass (walk sideways to the left), but this is an entirely different skill that is not covered in this definition.

## Prerequisites
None.

## Training Technique
The easiest way to teach your dog directional cues is to use them frequently while walking him on a leash in the *heel* position.

1. Teach *haw* and *gee* (also in this chapter) at the same time by issuing these commands a second before making a direction change to the left or right, respectively. Your dog will begin to anticipate the turns. Be sure to make full 90-degree turns so that it's obvious to him what the commands mean.

2. When you notice your dog anticipating the turns, start using the commands when he is walking ahead of you, either on a leash or in harness. He may look back at you for reassurance that he's going the correct way, and you can help him through this transition period by pointing with your finger in the direction you want to go. When he gains confidence, he'll begin making the turns without looking back.

# HIKE

## Description
This command instructs the dog to move forward at a run.

## Uses
Besides initiating the forward movement of sled dogs, this command can be useful any time you need to instruct your dog to

run on. If you jog with him, bicycle with him at your side, or enjoy a newer sport called scootering with him, *hike* is a good way to let him know when it's time to start running.

### Prerequisites
None.

### Training Technique
Your dog can quickly learn *hike* if you issue it consistently right before you launch on your expedition or any time you have to start out from a stop. Most dogs, especially those who love running, will react quickly to this command once they've associated it with running.

## HURRY UP (ALSO: BE QUICK)

### Description
This command encourages the dog to speed things up, especially when he's doing his business.

### Uses
This command can be used any time you want your dog to hurry up—when you're getting ready to leave somewhere, when you want him to finish a task like fetching,

The *hurry up* command encourages your dog to speed things up—use it when you're getting ready to leave somewhere, when you want him to finish a task, or when you want to quicken the pace during a walk.

or when you want him to quicken his pace while out for a walk. It is especially useful for dogs who are slowpokes!

### Prerequisites
None.

### Training Technique

1. The trick to teaching your dog this command lies in keeping pressure on him until he increases his pace, which may consist of constant verbal encouragement, clapping your hands, and generally acting impatient with his sluggishness. Discontinue the pressure when his speed increases. With consistent use of this command, he will soon understand what it means.

2. When using this command to encourage your dog to speed up his elimination habits, keep in mind that some dogs take longer to accomplish this task than others. You should not ask him to hurry up as long as he is focused on finding a spot to eliminate. Instead, use this command to direct him back to this task if he becomes distracted.

> Use the *in* command to instruct your dog to go into his kennel.

## IN

### Description
The dog goes through a door or entryway when instructed.

## Uses

*In* has many practical applications. You can instruct your dog to go into his kennel, into a vehicle, into a house, or into a room.

## Prerequisites

*Stay.*

## Training Technique

Before teaching your dog the *in* command, you'll need to decide if you'd rather use a more specific command in some situations. For instance, you can use the command *kennel* (see Chapter 9) to instruct him to go into his crate or the command *load up* (in this chapter) to instruct him to go to his special place in a vehicle. Make these decisions ahead of time so that you can be consistent in the specific command you use in each situation. You can then use the *in* command to apply to all other situations where your dog passes through a door.

## Without Food Rewards

1. Many dogs learn this command easily enough when their owners use it frequently and consistently. Let your dog know when you want him to pass through a doorway by pointing or waving your hand in the direction you want him to go while issuing an *in*.
2. Use the *stay* command to prevent your dog from getting into the habit of coming right back out after he's gone in. Release him with an *okay* if you want to allow him to come out. When you tell him *in*, he should stay in until

you tell him he can come out.

3. Use this command in every situation you want your dog to associate with it, such as going back into the house after playing outside and getting into the car. With practice, he will learn what this command means, and you can then stop waving your hand to direct him and start using the command alone.

## With Food Rewards

1. Sometimes dogs learn this command faster with food rewards, especially when the dog needs to learn to go into a kennel or other small spaces. Begin by throwing a treat just inside the doorway or kennel while issuing an *in*.
2. When your dog becomes comfortable retrieving a treat from just inside the doorway, start throwing the treat farther through the doorway until he starts passing completely through it.
3. At this point, you can begin making your dog stay after he's gone in. Do not allow him to come out unless you release him with an *okay* or *out* command.

## LEASH ON/LEASH OFF (ALSO: LEAD ON/LEAD OFF)

### Description

The dog stands still for his owner to put on or take off his leash.

### Uses

This is a great skill to teach a dog who fidgets while leashing up, and it is generally a nice heads up for your dog so

that he knows your intentions and what to expect.

## Prerequisites

*Stand/stay* or *sit/stay*.

## Training Technique

1. Consider teaching your dog to stand in a certain place for the *leash on* procedure, like right in front of the door or wherever you keep his leash. To do this, tell him to *stand* and *stay* (or *sit* and *stay*) at the location you choose, and then issue a *leash on* when you put on his leash. Make sure your dog goes to the same spot for *leash off*. Be consistent in using the same location every time you put on or take off his leash.

With *leash on* or *leash off*, the dog stands still for his owner to put on or take off his leash.

2. Do not allow your dog to break his stay until you give him a release cue like *okay*. It is the only way he will know when you have finished putting on or taking off his leash.

3. When your dog has had enough practice to know where he needs to go to get his leash on and off, try eliminating the *stand/stay* or *sit/stay* commands, and just issue a *leash on* or *leash off*.

# LET'S GO!

## Description
The dog leaves with his handler.

## Uses
This command is extremely useful in inspiring a dog to depart quickly. It basically means "Hurry up and come with me, I'm going somewhere," and the implication of travel and adventure motivates most dogs to respond enthusiastically. Use this command before walks to get your dog to assemble quickly for departure. Use it whenever you have paused during an outing and want to resume traveling. Use it any time you want to let your dog know he's invited to come with you.

## Prerequisites
None.

## Training Technique
1. Since *let's go!* has a built-in reward—the promise of travel—your dog only needs to learn what it means in order to respond appropriately to it.
2. Say these commands enthusiastically, and prod your dog to react quickly by clapping your hands and repeating the commands in rapid succession (verbal pressure) any time you plan to take your dog somewhere. It won't take long for him to connect let's go! with an immediate departure.

# LIFT (ALSO: LIFT PAW)

## Description
The dog lifts a foot so that his handler can untangle a leash from around his leg.

## Uses
This command is obviously useful when a dog steps over his leash, which is something that occurs frequently. It is much easier to untangle a leash or tie out when the dog willingly lifts his foot.

## Prerequisites
None.

## Training Technique
Because dogs tend to entangle their front legs more often than their back

---

## Exercising Before a Walk?

Most dogs like to get their leashes on because it means they get to go for a walk or embark on some other adventure. If your dog gets overexcited and won't stand still for you to get a leash on him, you may want to try Exercise First (in Chapter 4) to get him to settle down a bit. Then be very patient (and stubborn) about refusing to put his leash on unless he stands and stays for you. (Note: It may be too much to ask an excited dog for a *sit/stay*.) Your dog will soon learn that he can't go anywhere at all unless he cooperates.

---

legs, these training techniques focus on teaching your dog to lift his front legs.

1. Purposely allow your dog to step over his leash so that he can associate *lift* with a tangle situation.
2. Give the *lift* command, and tickle the back of your dog's leg just above his foot until he lifts it. (If this does not encourage him to lift his foot, try tickling the front of his toes.)
3. When your dog lifts his foot, pull the leash under it to untangle him and then issue a *good* to let him know he did what you wanted.
4. Repeat these steps until your dog begins to lift his foot at your command without your having to tickle him. Some dogs will become so proficient at this skill that they will automatically lift their foot when they feel a leash around their leg.

## LOAD UP

### Description
The dog gets into a vehicle and takes his proper place.

### Uses
This is a little more specific than the *in* command because the dog is expected to go to a specific seat, place on the floor, or in a travel kennel in the vehicle. This command can help minimize the distribution of dog hair in your vehicle and make it easier to use a doggy seatbelt or other canine vehicle restraint.

### Prerequisites
*Stay.*

### Training Technique
Your dog will learn this command easier and abide by it most consistently if you begin to use it as soon as you get him. If he falls into the habit of having the run of your vehicle's interior, it may be a little harder to get him to adopt a particular place in it.

1. Give the *load up* command and lead your dog to his place in the vehicle, then tell him to stay.
2. When this becomes a part of your dog's car-loading routine, you should be able to use the *load up* command without leading him—he'll know where to go.
3. If your dog resists going to his designated spot, refuse to go anywhere until he does. Most dogs love car rides and will comply in order to get on with the ride.

## PICK UP (FOR LITTLE DOGS)

### Description
The dog immediately comes close to his handler with the expectation of being picked up, or the dog jumps into his handler's arms.

### Uses
The purpose of this command is one of safety. Small dogs are at much greater risk of injury from larger dogs, inappropriate advances of children, or other dangerous situations. *Pick up* allows you to quickly retrieve your small dog into the safety of your arms. If you take this skill a step further and teach him to jump into your arms, it can also make a

fancy conclusion to any type of canine act or demonstration.

## Prerequisites

*Come.*

## Training Technique

In the case of a dangerous situation, you need your small dog to come to you immediately when you issue a *pick up*. It takes practice to achieve this kind of instant response, so practice the following training instructions frequently to condition him.

1. While out for a walk with your dog, call him to you occasionally with the *come* command. When he comes to you, issue a *pick up* and then pick him up. Encourage him to respond immediately with the use of verbal pressure in the form of rapidly and urgently repeating the *come* command and by clapping, stomping your feet, or whatever else you can do to get his immediate response. You can expedite this training by offering him a treat once he is in your arms.

2. When your dog appears to respond to your satisfaction, try to replace the *come* command with *pick up*. He

**Pick up** allows you to quickly retrieve your small dog into the safety of your arms.

should already be used to hearing you say this command right after *come*, so the transition should be easy. Practice *pick up* until he responds quickly the first time you say this command.

3. To get your dog to jump into your arms, all you need to do is call him to you with the *come* command, then hold a treat in the air close to you and encourage him to jump up to get it. When he jumps, scoop him out of the air into your arms! When you can get him to repeat this behavior several times, begin to label the behavior with the *pick up* command. Eventually, wean him off the *come* command and simply issue a *pick up* to instruct him what to do.

# SAY HI

## Description
The dog greets another dog politely.

## Uses
*Say hi* is a great way to socialize your dog with other dogs. Use it to help introduce him to a new family pet or dogs at the dog park. Use it to get him to settle down in the presence of other dogs.

## Prerequisites
None.

## Training Technique
*Say hi* is another way of saying, "Be nice." All

**Say hi** is a great way to socialize your dog with other animals. Use it to help introduce him to a new family pet or a dog at the park.

dogs should learn how to greet other dogs civilly without initiating skirmishes, barking inappropriately, or jumping all over a new canine acquaintance. It is best to introduce dogs to each other when both are on leashes, but take care not to let the dogs circle each other and become entangled.

Practice *say hi* with other friendly dogs you know so that your dog can learn what this command means. In real life, however, you may find there are some dogs with whom he just doesn't get along. Respect his choices in friends, and do not try to force him to be friends with a dog he doesn't like.

1. Allow your dog to approach a new dog and issue a *say hi*. Watch his behavior and body language closely so that you can interrupt an inappropriate greeting before it escalates.

2. If your dog shows signs of dominance, aggressiveness, or excessive excitement, issue an *uh-uh* and pull him away from the other dog. Give him time to settle down before attempting to introduce him again. Dogs generally like to greet each other, so depriving your dog of the opportunity to greet is punishment for inappropriate behavior.

3. If your dog behaves well for a greeting, give him about ten seconds to *say hi*, then issue an *okay, that's enough*, and pull him away. When he gets used to this greeting routine, he will begin to break off contact with new acquaintances willingly and without fuss.

# SWITCH (ALSO: CHANGE)

## Description

The dog circles behind his handler or ducks behind his handler's legs to switch from a *heel* position to a *foos* position or vice versa.

## Uses

This command is useful any time you need to switch your dog from one side to the other, such as when hazards or terrain make it necessary for him to walk on your opposite side. It is a good obedience or canine musical freestyle move, and you can also use it to untangle his leash from around your legs.

## Prerequisites

*Heel* and *foos*.

## Training Technique

There are two different ways to teach this maneuver to your dog. You can either teach him to duck behind your legs and come up on your other side, or you can teach him to circle away from you and come around behind you to your other side. The latter is a much more fluid motion if you want to use this maneuver in a canine musical freestyle routine.

If you want to teach your dog to switch in both directions, use a different command for each. For instance, use *switch* to tell him to switch from your left side to your right side, and use *change* to tell him to switch from your right side to your left side.

## To Duck Behind You

1. While walking with your dog in a *heel* position, issue a *switch* and lure him behind you to your other side by passing a treat behind your back from your left hand to your right hand. Make sure he stays forward-facing while making the switch, and continue to walk on as he moves to your other side.
2. When your dog comes up to your right side, issue a *yes!* and reward him. Then tell him to foos so that he maintains his position on your right side for a while before practicing the skill again.
3. Some dogs can learn both *switch* and *change* at the same time by luring them back and forth, but if your dog has difficulty with this, teach him one direction at a time.
4. When your dog appears to switch easily with a food lure, try it without one. Instead, use your finger to point behind your back when you issue a *switch*. If he does so, issue a *yes!* and reward him. If he doesn't, keep luring him until he's ready to switch at the verbal command and hand signal.

## To Circle Behind You

1. This maneuver is easier to teach from a standstill initially. With your dog in *heel* position at your right side (sitting or standing), tell him *switch* and lure him in a circle that turns away from you to the left and goes around your back. Pass the treat from your left hand to your right hand behind your back to get him to come around to your right side.

2. As soon as your dog comes up to your right side, issue a *yes!* and reward him.
3. Move to your dog's right side, and practice Steps 1 and 2 again. Repeat this exercise several times until he feels comfortable with it.
4. When your dog switches sides easily, it's time to practice this skill at a walk. Give your dog a *yes!* and a reward each time he circles correctly from your left to right side, and then make him maintain a *foos* position for a while before trying the skill again.
5. Again, you can teach *switch* and *change* at the same time by luring your dog back and forth, but be sure to make him heel or foos for a while before asking him to change his position again. If he has difficulty learning both skills at the same time, teach them separately.
6. Gradually fade your luring motions so that you can use your finger to make a semicircle motion that ends up pointing behind your back. This will become your hand signal for *switch*.

## THIS WAY

### Description
The dog looks at his handler to see which direction to go.

### Uses
This command is especially useful whenever your dog is walking ahead of you, whether on or off leash, because it allows you to tell him which way to

go. It is a very strong power command. Contrary to the popular belief that a canine leader must walk ahead of a dog to be in a position of control, the position of control belongs to whomever decides the direction of travel, regardless of who is walking first. (A human would find it nearly impossible to keep ahead of an off-leash dog when hiking trails or exploring anyway!)

## Prerequisites
*Come.*

## Training Technique
Do not teach your dog any off-leash skill unless he is proficient in the *come* command. *This way* can be a useful command for on-leash as well as off-leash dogs.

1. Get into the habit of giving the *this way* command every time you change directions while out for a walk with your dog, whether he's on or off leash. He will begin to look at you to see which direction you are going and will change his direction to match yours.

> Get into the habit of giving the *this way* command every time you change directions while out for a walk with your dog, whether he's on or off leash.

## TROT

### Description

The dog travels in a trotting (front right foot and rear left foot step at the same time and vice versa) or pacing (front and rear feet on the same side step at the same time) gait.

### Uses

The *trot* command helps to provide some speed control. It is useful if you like to jog, run, bicycle, or sled with your dog. You can teach this command as a companion to *run* (in Chapter 11) so that you can tell him exactly which gait you'd like him to have. This is also a good command to use to let him know you plan to increase your speed from a walk.

### Prerequisites

None.

### Training Technique

1. When out and about with your dog on a leash or harness, give the *trot* command and then encourage him to speed up into a trot. When he does, issue a *good* to let him know he's done the right thing.
2. If your dog speeds up into a run (gallop), issue an *uh-uh*, pull him back to slow him down into a trot, and tell him *trot* again. When he's taken a few trotting steps, tell him *good*. With consistent use of this command, he will learn that *trot* applies to this particular gait.

## WAIT UP

### Description

An off-leash dog who has run ahead stops and waits for his handler.

### Uses

This is a valuable power command you can use when out exploring trails with your dog, especially if he likes to run too far ahead. It can help keep him within a controllable distance and within sight when walking winding or hilly trails.

### Prerequisites

*Come* and *wait*.

### Training Technique

As an off-leash skill, *wait up* requires your dog to respond reliably to the *come* command. It also requires him to be responsive to his name.

Teach your dog the *wait* command from Chapter 9. It will then be easy for him to apply the skill of waiting for a moment in a *wait up* situation.

1. When your dog runs too far ahead, call his name to get his attention. This should cause him to stop and look at you. Then give the *wait up* command.
2. If your dog does not wait for you, or breaks his wait before you have released him, issue an *uh-uh* and call his name to get him to stop and pay attention to you again. Repeat the *wait up* command. You must be persistent at this point and insist that he stay where he is until you give him an *okay* to go on.

Use verbal pressure with insistent, commanding repetition, if necessary, to get him to comply.

3. When you have approached your dog within a reasonable distance, give him permission to proceed with an *okay*. Try to be consistent in the amount of distance between you and your dog when you issue the *okay* release so that he can learn what you consider to be an acceptable distance between you.

## WALK NICE

### Description
The dog stops pulling on his leash and walks appropriately.

### Uses
Obviously, the *walk nice* command is the foundation of good leash manners. It can save a handler plenty of neck, shoulder, back, and hand pain, and it can make dog walking a much more pleasurable activity.

*Wait up* is a valuable power command to use when out exploring trails with your dog, especially if he likes to run too far ahead.

### Prerequisites
None.

### Training Technique
*Walk nice* is not as disciplined as *heel* (in Chapter 7) because it simply requires the

dog to walk on a loose leash. The dog's position in relation to his handler is not important. However, be aware that dogs are easier to physically control when they are on a short leash rather than a long one. If your dog is a persistent puller, teach him *walk nice* on a short leash before granting him the privilege of walking on a longer leash.

It also helps to choose a consistent walking formation so that your dog can become accustomed to where he should be when he walks with you. For instance, insist that he always walk on your left side, even if he does not maintain a strict *heel* position.

1. Begin training in a place free of distractions, as you do not want stimuli like people or other animals to encourage your dog to pull. With him on leash, begin to walk.

2. If your dog pulls, stop abruptly and wait for him to turn and look at you. When he does so, it will put slack in the leash. Then issue a *walk nice* and start moving again.

3. Each time your dog pulls, repeat Step 2 until he understands that he can't go anywhere if he continues to pull. When he walks appropriately, occasionally tell him *good* to let him know you are pleased.

4. When your dog reliably performs *walk nice* in a

The *walk nice* command is the foundation of good leash manners.

distraction-free environment, start taking him on short walks to reinforce his lessons. Eventually, you can use *walk nice* as a warning when he temporarily forgets his leash manners.

## WALK ON (ALSO: ON BY)

### Description
The dog continues to walk on past a distraction.

### Uses
This is a particularly useful power command to employ when out walking with male dogs, as they like to stop and mark every vertical object along the way. If you are tired of having to stop at all the mailboxes in your neighborhood whenever you walk your dog, teach him *walk on*. It is also a good command to teach dogs who are strongly scent driven, as they like to stop and sniff everything. You can use this command to get your dog to walk past other distractions that he wants to stop and investigate as well, including other dogs, roadkill, and wild animals. The intent is to issue this command before he stops to investigate something so that you can keep him moving. If he has already stopped, use the *leave it* command from Chapter 9.

### Prerequisites
None.

### Training Technique
Dog walking is great exercise, but there is nothing more annoying than having your rhythm and pace interrupted every

## Leash Manners and Self-Control

Good leash manners are a matter of habit. Teach your dog how to walk nicely on leash before you start taking him for walks because it's too easy to allow him to get away with bad habits when distance or time constraints do not allow you to address inappropriate behaviors. In addition, pulling is one of the undesirable behaviors dogs engage in when they have too much energy to exercise self-control. If you have a high-energy dog, help him succeed by using Exercise First from Chapter 4 before going out and about. If he has considerable difficulty with the *walk nice* command, consider teaching him the more disciplined *heel* so that he can develop greater self-control.

few steps because your dog wants to stop and sniff something. A respectful, well-mannered dog doesn't stop for any reason unless his handler gives him permission to do so. Keep your dog in motion with the *walk on* command.

1. The trick to keeping your dog moving is to issue the *walk on* command before he becomes fixated on a distraction, as this helps to prepare his mind to ignore it. When walking him on leash, always look ahead to

try to identify distractions ahead of time. Also, observe him closely. If he appears to catch a whiff of something that he wants to investigate, get his attention with a verbal cue and then give the *walk on* command firmly and do not let him stop.

2. After your dog has had some practice and seems to be getting the hang of it, eliminate the verbal cue and only issue a *walk on*.

3. Keep your dog happy and willing to comply by offering him opportunities to do some sniffing now and then. Tell him *okay* when you want to allow sniffing. He will learn to stop and sniff only when you tell him he can.

## WHOA (ALSO: STOP)

### Description
The dog stops moving forward.

### Uses
This is a good command for sledders and carters to use to get their dogs to stop. You can use it while walking your dog to give him a heads up that you plan to stop. Use it to get him

The *whoa* command is useful for sledders who need their dogs to stop.

to stop chasing an animal, or any other time you need him to cease forward movement.

## Prerequisites
None.

## Training Technique
Always keep the purpose of a command in mind when teaching it to your dog. For instance, *whoa* should mean stop, not slow down. You cannot expect him to obey any command consistently if you do not use it consistently. So be sure to enforce a complete stop when teaching this command.

1. Consider teaching *whoa* in tandem with a command that inspires forward movement, like *hike* or *let's go!* (which are also in this chapter). Or use the *okay* command to release your dog from *whoa*. Employing a command with the opposite meaning of *whoa* will help him learn to distinguish between the two.

2. When you are out walking your dog on a leash, issue a *whoa* and then stop walking.

3. Maintain a *stop* for a few seconds. If your dog waits patiently, tell him *good*. If he fidgets, issue an *uh-uh*. After a few seconds, issue an *okay* to release him and start walking again.

4. Practice Steps 1 and 2 at least several times during every walk. Your dog will soon learn to stop at the *whoa* command.

Use *whoa* any time you need your dog to cease forward movement.

# 11

# PLAY AND ACTIVITIES

t may sound like all fun and games, but play and activities serve a very important purpose in your dog's life. Play helps to relieve stress and expend excess energy. It contributes to good mental and physical health. It helps develop strong bonds with family members. And believe it or not, playtime with your dog provides these exact same benefits for *you*. So do not let time constraints convince you to neglect spending healthy quality time with him.

It's important to designate a specific time each day to play with and exercise your dog—his welfare and good behavior depend on it. Remember, a happy dog is a well-behaved dog. Not only does regular exercise and activity help him expend his energy in appropriate and productive ways, it helps regulate his sleeping and elimination patterns to prevent nighttime disturbances and house soiling accidents.

Besides providing the aforementioned benefits—which are substantial—many play and activity commands have practical uses beyond their face value. For example, *drop it* can help you get your dog to give up a potentially harmful item he's picked up while on a walk. *Fetch* may very well progress from a typical game to a

*Catch* **can prove to be a test of endurance if you count the number of balls your dog catches without dropping or missing one.**

helpful household skill. And *get your toy* can help resolve a jumping problem. Of all the commands covered in this book, not one is trivial or useless if used to its greatest potential.

# CATCH

## Description

The dog catches an object in his mouth (e.g., ball, disk, or food) before it hits the floor.

## Uses

Taken to the extreme, it can become an amazing test of skill when a dog catches an object that is thrown high into the air or lobbed far away on command. Catch can prove to be a test of endurance if you count the number of balls your dog catches without dropping or missing one.

## Prerequisites

None.

## Training Technique

Some dogs are natural catchers and pick up this skill very quickly, but others need more practice to become experts at it.

1. To make it easy for your dog to get the hang of snatching flying objects in midair, start out at a short distance from him and use an object or treat that is highly motivating.
2. Give the *catch* command, and throw the object into the air in a gentle arc— this keeps the object in the air longer, giving your dog more time to make the catch.

## Catch Advantages

The *catch* command can come in handy during training because the handler can deliver treats much quicker whenever there is a distance separating her from the dog. It can also help prevent fingers from getting nipped while delivering treats to an overexuberant canine pupil or athlete.

3. Gradually increase the distance of your throws as your dog gains proficiency in catching. You can also begin to throw higher or faster, depending on how well he advances. Use *catch* as a heads-up warning rather than a command. Soon, your dog will snap to attention when he hears this command and will be ready for any incoming food or toy bombs.

# DROP IT (ALSO: GIVE)

## Description

The dog lets go of something in his mouth. He may learn to drop an item onto the ground or into his owner's hand.

## Uses

In less critical situations, it can help manage a dog who likes to steal your possessions or chew on inappropriate objects. It is also the third in a sequence of behaviors to get a dog to take, hold, and drop an item. (*Take it* and *hold*, which are covered later in this chapter, are

power commands; they require the dog to relinquish something [resources] he has in his possession.)

## Prerequisites

*Take it* and *hold* (only for the *take it/hold/drop it* sequence).

## Training Technique

Some dogs have exceptionally strong possession tendencies and may even become aggressive if you try to take what they consider to be theirs. Because of this, it's important not to physically force a dog to relinquish his prize. Furthermore, be cautious when attempting to retrieve something your dog views as extremely high in value, especially food items. If he shows possession aggression with toys, bed space, or anything else, obtain professional assistance before teaching *drop it*.

Owners most often use the *drop it* command to get a dog to release a toy when engaged in play. But it can also be a lifesaver when he gets hold of a hazardous or toxic item.

To get your dog to relinquish what he possesses, you must offer him a deal; that is, you need to give him an option that appeals to him as much or more than keeping what he possesses. The specific option may differ from one situation to another, but it always involves presenting him with something desirable in place of the item in his mouth.

## Dog Toys

Dogs are notorious for refusing to give up their balls and flying disks, which can quickly put an end to a game of fetch. They may like to hang onto their prizes, but they also tend to think the prizes of others are always better than their own— call it "the grass is always greener on the other side of the fence" syndrome. Because of this, the easiest way to encourage your dog to drop it is to tease him with a second ball or toy. He will willingly drop his prize to pursue yours.

1. Give the *drop it* command when you tease your dog with a ball or flying disc, and then issue a *good* when he does so. Throw the second ball or flying disc as a reward for his compliance. Soon he will respond consistently to *drop it*.

2. Use this same technique to get your dog to drop any of his other toys as well, as long as you can offer him another toy of equal or greater value to him. If you practice *drop it* while holding your hand under his mouth, you can teach him to drop his toys directly into your hand.

## Inappropriate Items

If your dog refuses to drop his toys, it probably would not be a huge catastrophe; but if he gets a mouthful of toxic plant leaves, it's important for him to heed the *drop it* command. Less dangerous but equally annoying, some dogs get into the habit of stealing children's toys. Some like to chew on shoes or socks. Some, as disgusting as it seems to humans, love to snack on tidbits from the cat's litter box. Practicing *drop it* with your dog's toys can help prepare him to respond to this command in other situations.

1. Occasionally, when your dog is playing with one of his toys, say *drop it* and offer him another toy or a food reward in exchange for the one in his mouth. When he willingly relinquishes his toy, reward him with a little playtime or a food reward.

2. When your dog understands the meaning of *drop it*, you can use

## Possessive Tendencies

A dog's instinct to hang onto anything he picks up in his mouth is directly related to primitive canine feeding practices. In the wild, survival depends on getting a share of the pack's kill and keeping it. Vestiges of these feeding instincts are evident in a dog's love of playing tug (wild canines often tug over the same scrap of food), the tendency to gulp food or take it from his dish to another location to eat it (wild canines do these things to avoid competition with pack mates), and the reluctance to give up what he has in his mouth (possession is nine-tenths of the law in the dog world).

this command to stop him from chewing on inappropriate items. Always be sure to give him something acceptable to chew in place of the forbidden item.

3. Situations may arise in which you do not have a toy or food reward to trade. In most such cases, your dog will obey you as long as you have taught him the meaning of *drop it* and he has learned to respect you as a canine leader. Don't forget to take precautions to prevent him from getting hold of unsafe items, and teach the *leave it* command from Chapter 9 as a precaution.

## As Part of the Take It/Hold/Drop It Sequence

1. Once your dog has learned take it and hold, he will most likely learn drop it simply from its context (if he already has something in his mouth, the next logical step is for him to drop it) or from your body language (your extended hand makes it obvious you want him to drop the item in your hand).

2. The presentation of a food reward is usually sufficient to convince a dog to comply if he is reluctant to drop something because he cannot hold the item in his mouth and eat a treat at the same time!

## FETCH (ALSO: GET IT)

### Description
The dog retrieves a specific item indicated by his handler.

### Uses
This command is exceptionally handy in many situations, and yet it is highly underused and underappreciated. *Fetch* is not just a game; it's a job. Imagine having a dog who will pick up dirty socks from the floor and put them in a laundry basket. Imagine having a dog who will pick up your dropped keys, fetch your newspaper, or bring your slippers to you. The applications of *fetch* are limitless!

### Prerequisites
None.

### Training Technique
Dogs who enjoy retrieving are especially good at fetching.

1. Before your dog can learn to fetch an object, he must be willing to put it in his mouth. Tease him with the object by waving it in front of him and encouraging him to grab it. If he grabs it or picks it up in his mouth, issue a *yes!* and give him a food reward.

2. When your dog understands that you want him to take the object in his mouth, you can begin to teach him to retrieve it. Roll the object on the floor, encourage him to get it with *fetch*, and then hold your hand under his mouth to catch the item when he drops it. He will gladly release it when you produce a food reward because dogs can't hold objects in their mouths and eat food at the same time.

3. The next step is to teach your dog to retrieve the object without having to entice him by rolling or throwing it. By now, he already knows that *fetch*

means to grab and drop an object. Start placing the object on the ground, point to it, and ask your dog to fetch. Hold your hand out to catch it when he drops it.

4. Increase the distance between you and the object. Take a couple steps away from it, point to it, instruct your dog to fetch, and only reward him when he drops it in your outstretched hand. Gradually increase the distance until he fetches it from across the room. When working with pairs of objects, like slippers, wait until your dog fetches one item reliably, and then introduce the second one. Instruct him to *fetch*, and when he returns with one item, send him back to get the second one before you reward him.

5. Depending on the object you've taught your dog to fetch, you may need to practice fetching it from the place it's normally located. For example, you might keep your slippers under the bed, your shoes by the front door, or your cell phone on the end table. You can even teach him to fetch the newspaper from your porch.

6. In situations where you will not be able to point to the object because it's usually located in another room (or outside), you'll have to use the object's name instead of the word

*Fetch* is not just a game; it's a job. Imagine having a dog who will fetch your newspaper or bring your slippers to you on command!

*fetch* so that your dog knows what you want him to retrieve. Place the item in its usual location and stand by a doorway where you can see it when you ask him to fetch it. Eventually move farther through the doorway into another room until the object is no longer visible when you send him to fetch it. This skill may takes lots of practice, but there is double the joy in owning a dog who is as helpful as he is fun.

## Fetch Fussiness

Some dogs are a bit particular about what they will put in their mouths. Your dog may be less than enthusiastic about fetching metallic, gritty, or stringy objects, and there's no need to force him to do it. There are plenty of other items you can teach him to fetch, such as cell phones, remote controls, and shoes. If you plan to teach your dog to fetch more than one type of item, you'll have to use the name of the items in place of the word *fetch* so that he can distinguish among them. Also, be aware that a dog's teeth can do damage, especially if he has a hard mouth. Protective sleeves for phones and remotes will not only prevent damage, they can also make them more mouth-worthy for your dog.

# FIND IT (ALSO: GO FIND)

## Description
The dog finds a hidden treat by scent.

## Uses
This game is particularly appealing to dogs who have a strong scenting drive—use it to stimulate and satisfy your dog's natural instincts! It can also become a fun trick that impresses your friends, or it can provide a good example of a dog's scenting ability for public demonstrations.

## Prerequisites
*Sit*.

## Training Technique
Assemble several (three or four) containers with lids. These should be opaque so that your dog can't see what's inside of them. (Plastic butter containers from the recycle bin work well.) Punch holes in the lids so that he will be able to smell the contents.

1. Put a treat inside one of the containers. When teaching and performing *find it*, be very careful not to get the treat scent on the empty containers, as this will confuse your dog.
2. Get your dog excited about finding the treat by letting him sniff the container with the treat in it and then opening it and letting him eat it.
3. Arrange all the containers on the floor in a straight line about 4 feet (1.25 m) apart from each other.
4. With your dog on a leash, give the *find it* command and walk him past the

containers, encouraging him to sniff each one for the treat. If he shows any interest or hesitation at the container that contains the treat, issue a *sit*. Then say *yes!* and reward him. The *sit* will become your dog's alert to let you know when he's found the correct container.

5. Do not discourage your dog from pawing at or nosing the container with the treat, but wait until he sits before giving him a *yes!* and a reward.

   With practice, your dog will learn the sequence of what he must do to earn a reward: Find the right container and then sit. Dogs who love scenting will pick this up quickly and perform it enthusiastically.

The *find it* game can be a fun activity for dogs with a strong scenting drive.

## Variations

Here are two more games you can try with your dog.

1. To test your dog's true scenting abilities, try rubbing the treat inside a container instead of actually putting it inside, and see if your dog can still find the correct container.

2. Another fun *find it* game consists of hiding treats in a room and turning

your dog loose to find them. Just for fun, time him and see how long it takes him to locate them all.

## GET YOUR TOY

### Description
The dog gets his toy when instructed to do so.

### Uses
This is a variation of *fetch* that focuses on your dog's playthings. Although *get your toy* is a great way to initiate play with him, it's useful in many other situations as well. You can use *get your toy* to redirect him away from engaging in an undesirable behavior, such as jumping up or barking (always issue a displeasure cue like *uh-uh* before redirecting him). It can also become an impressive trick if you replace *toy* with the names of specific toys and teach him to fetch the individual items.

> The *get your toy* command can be used to redirect your dog away from engaging in an undesirable behavior, such as jumping up or barking.

### Prerequisites
None.

### Training Technique
Toy fetching is relatively easy to teach because it's hard to find a dog who

doesn't love to play with toys. However, since most dogs do not have the patience to search the entire house to find their favorite playthings, it is best to have a central location or toy box to keep them in. Then when you tell your dog to get his toy, he'll know where to find it.

1. Start out with your dog's favorite toy. If you keep his toys in a toy box, make sure it is right on top. Point to it and give the *get your toy* command. (If you plan to teach your dog to fetch different toys, use the name of his favorite toy instead of the word "toy.") If he is in a playful mood, he'll grab it readily. If he doesn't, tease him with it until he takes it in his mouth. Reward him with a short play session if he grabs it.

2. When your dog willingly and reliably grabs his toy on command, stand a little farther away from it when asking him to get it. Again, reward him with a short play session if he fetches it.

3. Gradually increase the distance between yourself and the toy each time you ask your dog to get it until he fetches it no matter where you are whenever you ask him to get it.

4. To teach your dog to retrieve other toys by name, go through the above training steps with each item. Make sure he has completely mastered the first item before moving onto the next, and so on. This means he should consistently fetch the correct item by name before introducing a new one.

# HOLD (ALSO: HOLD IT)

## Description
The dog holds an item in his mouth until told to drop it.

## Uses
This is a very versatile trick because you can teach your dog to hold just about anything in his mouth you'd like. He can hold a wrench while you fix the plumbing under the sink. He can hold a basket of gifts when you visit the nursing home. He can hold a flower to impress your sweetheart. The practical uses are endless.

## Prerequisites
*Take it*.

## Training Technique
Again, keep in mind that dogs can be a little fussy about what they hold in their mouths. Some won't like to hold hard metal items like tools against their teeth. Others won't want to hold very fluffy things in their mouths. Don't force your dog to tolerate something that is uncomfortable for him. In certain cases, you can wrap cloth or tape around an object to make it more palatable for him. Teach *take it* (also in this chapter) first. Then you can begin to teach him to hold an item in his mouth for longer periods of time.

1. With the item in your dog's mouth, give the *hold* command, and use the same hand signal you would use for a *stay* (palm facing your dog). Require him to hold it for only a second before

issuing a *yes!* and rewarding him. He will automatically drop it to eat his food reward.

2. Require your dog to hold the item for successively longer periods of time before issuing a *yes!* and rewarding him.

3. When your dog will hold an item for as long as you desire, you can start teaching him the *drop it* command (also in this chapter).

## JUMP (ALSO: OVER)

### Description
The dog jumps over something when instructed to do so.

### Uses
This command has too many uses to list. It is often used in the sports of canine musical freestyle and agility, and it also makes an impressive trick. Teach your dog to jump through a hoop, over your arm or leg, or over an obstacle. Teach him to jump over puddles when you're out walking. One dog owner even used this command to instruct her dog how to jump against

*Hold* is a very versatile trick because you can teach your dog to hold just about anything in his mouth—like flowers to impress your sweetheart!

high waves at the beach when visiting the ocean!

## Prerequisites
None.

## Training Technique
Jumping is an especially athletic activity, so make sure your dog is physically capable of performing it. Never ask him to jump heights that could result in injury! The sport of agility provides reasonable limits on jump heights based on the heights of dogs, and these are good guidelines to follow.

1. Training usually begins by teaching the dog to jump over some type of object. Use something with an adjustable height. A hula-hoop, wooden dowel, or floor-standing item like an agility jump works well.

2. Start out with the jump at a very low height, and lure your dog over it with a treat while giving the *jump* command. Initially, he should be able to step over the jump at a walk. Issue a *yes!* and reward him with the treat when he crosses it.

3. Gradually raise the jump higher and higher so that your dog can become comfortable going over greater heights, saying *yes!* and rewarding him each time he crosses it successfully.

4. Once your dog is actually jumping over the jump and appears to know what you expect of him, you can begin to point at it instead of luring him over it.

5. You may need to repeat some or all of these training steps for each type of jump you want your dog to master. If you expose him to more than one type, he is more likely to generalize the *jump* command so that when you encounter a log across a hiking trail, for example, he will understand what you want him to do.

# PULL (ALSO: TUG)

## Description
The dog pulls on or plays tug with an item designated by his handler.

## Uses
Besides initiating a good game of tug-of-war, *pull* has many practical applications. You can use it to teach your dog to pull open doors and cabinets to which you have tied a tug rope or rag. He can pull kids on a sled, turn on lights with pull chains, or pull a bell rope to let you know he has to go outside. He can even pull off your socks and shoes for you. Use your imagination!

## Prerequisites
None.

## Training Technique
Depending on the item you want your dog to pull, it may help to teach him *take it* (also in this chapter) first. Also note that some dogs enjoy tugging more than others. Keep your dog's individual talents in mind when considering whether or not to teach him this command.

1. If your dog already enjoys tugging, he can learn this command relatively quickly if you offer him a tug toy he already enjoys playing with. Give the *pull* command, and let him tug on it.

2. After repeating Step 1 enough times for your dog to get a basic understanding of the command, try replacing the tug toy with something else, like a rope or rag. He may be particular about what he does and doesn't like to put in his mouth, so work with his preferences. When teaching him to tug on new objects, issue a *yes!* and reward him whenever he does what you want.

3. Once your dog understands this command and will tug on various objects, you can try to get him to tug on just about anything by teasing him with it playfully and issuing a *pull.*

## RUN (ALSO: GO, GO, GO!)

### Description

The dog runs when instructed to do so.

Besides initiating a good game of tug-of-war, *pull* has many practical applications. You can use it to teach your dog to pull open doors and cabinets to which you have tied a tug rope.

### Uses

The *run* command is a great way to encourage your dog to get a good workout during exercise time. It can also encourage sled dogs to run harder. Use it to spur your dog on during lure coursing (a chasing sport), herding, or agility. Any time you want him to step on the gas, *run* will help accomplish the task.

## Prerequisites
None.

## Training Technique
Since the purpose of *run* is to get your dog juiced up for running, always say it in an enthusiastic, encouraging way.

1. In the beginning, always issue the *run* command when your dog is already excited and running. Encourage him to increase his speed by clapping your hands or chasing him.
2. When you notice that your dog consistently shows increased eagerness and speed whenever you give the *run* command, begin to use it at times when he is not running to get him into a running mood.

# SEEK (ALSO: SEARCH)

## Description
The dog tracks a scent or locates a particular scent.

## Uses
This skill is a more professional version of the *find it* game. You can train your dog to locate missing persons or lost pets. These same techniques are often used to train dogs in all kinds of scent work, including bomb and narcotics detection. What do you want your dog to find?

## Prerequisites
None.

## Training Technique
Tracking and locating a scent are actually two different types of scent work, so different training methods for each are explained here. Also, teaching a dog to track competitively is beyond the scope of this book. The following training techniques will allow you to participate in fun scenting activities at home with your dog.

## Tracking a Scent
You will need a tracklayer (someone who leaves a trail for your dog to follow). You may also want to purchase a tracking harness and line, which will allow you to keep control of your dog without interfering with him as he works the track.

1. To start, lay a simple, straight track in a grassy area. The tracklayer should leave one item, like a glove, with her

### Search and Rescue
Search and rescue organizations may use training methods that are different from the ones described in this book. If you are interested in doing scent work professionally, contact the search and rescue group that operates in your area and participate in its training program. If you are interested in volunteering with your dog, visit the National Association for Search and Rescue website at www.nasar.org for information.

scent on it at the beginning of the track for your dog to smell. Another scented item should be left along the track for him to find. Have the tracklayer put a treat in every second or third footprint along the track, and make sure there is a treat inside or under the scent item along the track, too.

2. With the tracklayer out of your dog's sight, give the *seek* command and encourage him to follow the trail of treats.

3. When your dog begins to understand how this game works, start spacing the treats out in every fourth or fifth footprint. Then, as he progresses, space them out even more. This will force your dog to start following the tracklayer's scent, rather than the scent of treats, to find his food rewards. There should always be a reward and plentiful praise when he makes it to the end of a track.

The *seek* command is used for scenting and tracking. It's a skill that can help rescue teams locate missing persons or lost pets.

**4.** After your dog shows some proficiency in following the scent on a simple track, ask the tracklayer to start making the tracks a little more complicated, with one or two turns. (You may want these to be marked with flags.) Always watch your dog for signs that he may have lost the scent so that you can help him get back on course. With practice, he will become an excellent tracking dog.

## Locating a Scent

This kind of scent work would be used mainly for recreational purposes.

**1.** The first step in teaching your dog to locate a scent is to decide what kind of scent you want him to find. Maybe you want to teach him to find people so that you can play hide-and-seek.

Maybe you want him to sniff out cell phones or iPods because you keep misplacing yours.

**2.** The second decision you need to make concerns the type of alert your dog will give. Do you want him to display an aggressive alert by scratching and pawing at the site of a scent? Or do you want him to display a passive alert by sitting down as soon as he detects the scent? You might base this decision on his natural reaction to scent work (an exceptionally enthusiastic dog will automatically paw at a scent location) or the type of scent detection you teach him (you

Try teaching your dog how to sniff out your cell phone or keys if you often misplace them.

may not want your dog to paw at your cell phone and break it).

## Hide-and-Seek

To search for people, have a family member hide somewhere. The hider should have treats ready to give your dog when he finds her.

1. Tell your dog *seek*, and have the hider call him. Reward and praise him when he finds the hider. It should only take a few repetitions for him to learn the joys of this game.
2. Next, the hider can stop calling your dog, and he can try to locate the person on his own when you tell him *seek*.

## Locating a Cell Phone or Other Item

1. Wrap the scent object in a rag along with a treat, and leave it on the floor.
2. With your dog on a leash, tell him *seek* and walk him past the object.
3. If he shows any interest in it, say *yes!* and let him have the treat.
4. Repeat Steps 1 through 3 until your dog understands that *seek* means he should seek out the particular scent item with which you're working. At this point, you can begin to encourage him to paw it before you reward him, or tell him to sit before you reward him, depending on which type of alert you want him to give.
5. Start making it more difficult for your dog to find the object. Stick it between the cushions of your couch, under the bed, or behind furniture.
6. Up until this point, your dog has been seeking out the scent of the

treat, and it's time to transition him to searching for the scent object instead. Continue to wrap it in a rag that has a treat scent on it, but do not put a treat in it. You want to diminish the scent of the treat until there is only the scent of the object you've asked him to find.
7. When your dog consistently finds the scent object with only a faint scent of a treat in it, challenge him to find it wrapped in a rag that has no treat scent at all. Make the item relatively easy to find to help your dog succeed. If he shows any interest in it at all, say *yes!* and reward him.
8. Practice until your dog consistently locates the scent object, and then start hiding it by itself, without a rag wrapped around it. When he masters locating the item by itself, you have successfully trained your personal detection dog!

# TAKE IT

## Description
The dog takes an item in his mouth when instructed to do so.

## Uses
Use this command to encourage your dog to play with a toy. Teach it along with the *hold* command (also in this chapter) so that he can learn to assist you by holding things. Use it to help train him to do other skills, like *open the door* (in Chapter 12).

## Prerequisites
None.

## Training Technique

Consider teaching *take it*, *hold*, and *drop it* (all located in this chapter) in sequence to make this a more useful skill.

1. Begin by offering your dog something you know he will willingly take in his mouth, like a tug toy or bone. Give the *take it* command and encourage him by teasing him with it.

2. When your dog takes the item in his mouth, say *yes!* and give him a food reward. He will automatically drop the item in his mouth to accept the food. Practice Steps 1 and 2 until he appears to understand what you want him to do when you issue a *take it*.

3. Then you can begin to substitute other items you'd like to teach your dog to take. At first it is important to offer items he is not averse to taking in his mouth because he may begin to refuse to take anything at all if the training becomes too uncomfortable for him.

4. Once your dog will take things in his mouth on command, you can teach him to hold things in his mouth for longer periods of time with the *hold* command. Again, it helps to initiate these additional phases of training using items he is exceptionally willing to take.

> The *take it* command encourages your dog to play with a toy.

# 12

# TRICKS

**D**ogs have been endearing themselves to humans for thousands of years, and if there is one canine characteristic that has helped them do so, it would have to be their entertainment value! They have been performing tricks for us perhaps since the very first companion dog did something that amused his owner. Since then, we have been training them to amuse us on purpose. But trick training is not frivolous by any means. Like all the other commands in this book, trick commands can have alternative, practical uses. Some allow your dog to help you around the house. Others can be used as icebreakers at parties. They can be incorporated into canine musical freestyle routines, or they can be included in public demonstrations or therapy dog work.

Pet ownership should add enjoyment and enrichment to your life, and trick training can definitely fulfill this purpose. Your dog, likewise, will benefit from it because he will enjoy all the attention he gets out of amusing you. If he is treat motivated, there is no limit to what you can teach him. People will be amazed at how smart he is!

As with any other training endeavors, keep your dog's natural talents in mind, and be observant of the behaviors he offers on his own. If you catch him doing something cute or entertaining, you may be able to get him to repeat the behavior if you offer him a treat to do so. Trick training allows you to discover your dog's individual talents and cultivate them for their true potential.

## ACHOO

### Description
The dog pulls a handkerchief out of the handler's pocket when he hears a sneeze.

### Uses
This is a very impressive trick that is exceptionally easy to teach a dog who likes to fetch or tug.

### Prerequisites
None.

### Training Technique
Since this trick requires the dog to pull on a handkerchief with his mouth, you may want to keep several handkerchiefs on hand to replace ones that get torn.

1. First, wave the handkerchief in front of your dog and tease him with it to encourage him to grab it and tug on

### Kids and Trick Training
Any type of training, including trick training, helps you to develop a stronger bond and better communication with your dog. Trick training can also be a fun activity for children, giving them good experience in properly interacting with animals that will last a lifetime. It is a great way to bring kids and pets together and encourage them to develop their own close relationships.

it. When he does, issue a *yes!* and reward him.

2. When your dog has no problem grabbing and pulling on the handkerchief, stick one end of it in your pocket and tease him with the loose end. If he grabs and pulls on it, issue a *yes!* and reward him. Practice this until he consistently pulls the handkerchief all the way out of your pocket.

3. You can then begin issuing a fake sneeze right before you tease your dog with the end of the handkerchief. With repetition, he will learn that the sneeze is his cue to pull it from your pocket.

4. The finishing touch on this trick is to get your dog to give you the handkerchief after he pulls it from your pocket. Encourage him to put it in your hand before you give him a *yes!* and a reward. If this is difficult for him, consider teaching him the *drop it* command in Chapter 11.

## BALANCE THE BISCUIT (ALSO: BALANCE)

### Description
The dog balances a dog biscuit on his nose until he's given permission to eat it. Many dogs learn to flip the biscuit around

*Balance the biscuit is a fun way to make your dog earn a treat without simply giving it to him.*

their snouts and into their mouths, which makes an even more impressive trick.

## Uses
This is a fun way to make your dog earn a treat without simply giving it to him.

## Prerequisites
*Sit* and *stay*.

## Training Technique
Although you can certainly teach your dog the *balance the biscuit* command, many people prefer to use a *stay* to instruct their dogs to sit still with a biscuit on their nose. If you choose to use *balance* or *balance the biscuit*, use the same drawn-out tone of voice you would use with *stay*.

1. With your dog sitting, hold his muzzle steady and place a dog biscuit crossways on his nose for just a second or two. Instruct him to stay, and keep your hands close to the biscuit to prevent him from dropping it or snatching it prematurely. If he succeeds in holding his position, issue an *okay* to release him from the *stay* and allow him to eat the biscuit.
2. As you practice this skill, ask your dog to maintain his *stay* for successively longer periods of time.

# BEG (ALSO: SIT PRETTY)

## Description
The dog balances in a seated position with his front paws held up off the ground.

## Uses
Use this trick to create a double *high five* or a *stick 'em up*, especially if your dog tends to lift his paws straight up into the air when he performs the *beg* command. Combine this trick with *balance the biscuit* (in this chapter) to make an even more impressive trick. Maintaining a *beg* can also make it easier to groom his underside.

## Prerequisites
*Sit*.

## Training Technique
Some dogs may find the *beg* position difficult and uncomfortable due to their conformation. In addition, it may put undue stress on the vertebrae of long-backed dogs like Dachshunds and Basset Hounds. Keep these things in mind when deciding to teach this skill.

1. With your dog in a sitting position, hold a treat above his head, just behind his eyes, and barely out of his reach. (You may have to hold the treat in a closed hand to prevent him from snatching it.)
2. When your dog lifts his front feet off the ground in an attempt to reach the treat, issue a *yes!* and let him have the reward. If he tries jumping to get the treat, you may be holding it too high.
3. Gradually require your dog to maintain a *beg* position for a few seconds longer before saying *yes!* and allowing him to have the treat.
4. When your dog is sitting up to your satisfaction, you may begin to use the

beg command whenever you want him to adopt this position. You can also begin to hold the treat farther from his head until he learns to respond to just the gesture of your hand rather than a treat over his head.

## BOW

### Description
The dog's front end assumes a *down* position while his rear end remains standing, a position known as a play bow.

### Uses
The *bow* command is a nice finishing touch to any trick or routine, and it is easier to teach than most people think.

### Prerequisites
None.

### Training Technique
Although there are no prerequisites for this trick, *stand* from Chapter 8 may be a helpful preliminary skill in some cases.

> The *bow* is a nice finishing touch to any trick or routine. The dog's front end assumes a *down* position while his rear end remains standing.

1. With your dog standing on your left side (*heel* position), kneel next to him and try to lure his front end down to the floor by holding a treat on the ground in front of him with your right hand. Place your left arm under his belly, just in front of his rear legs, to assist him in keeping his rear end in the air. If he drops his front end to get

the treat, even just a little bit, issue a *yes!* and let him have the treat.

2. Keep practicing this skill, gradually drawing the treat farther away from your dog with the goal of eventually getting him to drop his front end low enough so that his elbows touch the floor. At this point, begin to use the *bow* command so that he associates it with the *bow* position.

3. Next, get your dog to relinquish his dependency on your left arm for assistance. Each time you give the *bow* command, keep your left arm under him just in case, but be careful not to touch him unless absolutely necessary. If he completes a *bow* without any physical help from you, he deserves a *yes!* as well as a reward and plenty of praise. Eventually, you can withdraw your left arm completely, and he will be bowing like a professional performing pooch!

## CIRCLE (ALSO: AROUND)

### Description
This command instructs the dog to walk in a clockwise direction around his handler.

### Use
Besides providing a simple dance move in canine musical freestyle, this command is a good way to get a dog into the *heel* position in lieu of a *come 'round* command. It also comes in handy to untangle a leash when a dog has gotten on the wrong side of his handler.

### Prerequisites
*Front.*

### Training Technique
In the sport of canine musical freestyle, opposite movements have separate names. In this case, if you use the *circle* command for your dog's clockwise movement around your body, you might use the *around* command to designate a counterclockwise movement. You can teach your dog one or both directions by using food rewards to lure him.

1. With your dog in a *front* position (standing, facing you), tell him *circle*. Use a treat to lure him around your body in a clockwise direction. Pass the treat from one hand to the other behind your back, and bring it back in front of you to get your dog to return to a *front* position.

2. When your dog completes the circle, issue a *yes!* and reward him. Most dogs learn this maneuver quickly, but to avoid confusing him, do not teach the opposite *around* until he performs the *circle* perfectly and consistently. You can also practice circles from the *heel* position (and practice *around* from the opposite *foos* position). If you have a high-energy dog, he'll literally be running circles around you!

## CLOSE THE DOOR (ALSO: CLOSE, SHUT THE DOOR)

### Description
The dog pushes a door shut with his nose or paws.

## Uses

This is a great skill to teach your dog if you have limited mobility and would like to train him to provide physical assistance, but it can be a great help in just about any situation.

## Prerequisites

*Touch.*

## Training Technique

This skill is a complex behavior that involves several stages of training to achieve the desired result. Like humans, dogs sometimes have to learn to walk before they can run. The first step in training this skill is to teach the dog to push the door in the direction it closes.

The second step is to teach him to push the door all the way shut. And the third step is to teach him to move the door into a position in which he can push it shut.

The first step in training *close the door* is to teach your dog to push the door in the direction it closes.

1. Choose a particular door with which to conduct your training. In the beginning, leave the door open just a crack. Stand behind it, and encourage your dog to put his paws up on it by holding a treat against it. Hold the treat high enough so that it will be at his nose level if he stands on his hind legs to get it. Some dogs may resist putting their feet on the door, but

encourage your dog enthusiastically to stay on his hind legs, and he may eventually put a paw against the door for balance.

2. The instant your dog puts a paw on the door, issue a *yes!* and give him the reward. Abundant praise is in order if he succeeds in moving the door closer to a shut position.

3. When your dog understands that you want him to put his feet on the door, gradually move into phase two of training. Require him to put more and more pressure against the door before giving him his reward. The goal is to get him to shut the door until the doorknob clicks; he will eventually recognize that click as the successful completion of his job. This is the point when you can start using the *close the door* command to tell

him what you want him to do. If your door is particularly difficult for him to close, try lubricating the hinges and the doorknob mechanism. More than likely, you don't leave your doors ajar as a matter of practice, so you'll have to teach your dog how to close the door when it's wide open.

4. The third phase of training involves gradually opening the door wider and wider each time you ask your dog to close it. The key to success with this skill is taking each of these increments slowly and making sure he is proficient at each level before moving on.

5. As a finishing touch, you can teach your dog how to nuzzle his nose behind the door so that he can get it into a position to push it closed. With the door completely opened, put a treat behind it and encourage him to get it. He'll automatically push the door away from the wall when he wedges his body behind it to get the treat. Then immediately give the *close the door* command. If you practice and repeat this sequence of behaviors enough times, he will begin to perform them together smoothly.

6. When your dog has fully mastered *close the door*, you can practice on other doors in your home. No more getting out of bed in the middle of the night to shut the bedroom door!

## CRAWL (ALSO: CREEP)

### Description
The dog crawls along on the floor on his belly.

## Uses

Although it's fun to watch a dog crawl on his belly, you never know when such a skill will come in handy—it may help your dog get out of a tight spot, win a limbo contest at the local pet fair, or contribute to a dramatic performance when combined with a *play dead* trick.

## Prerequisites

*Down.*

## Training Technique

This is a fairly simple trick to teach your dog, but it will get a lot of wows from those who are sure to be impressed with his amazing abilities.

1. Start with your dog in a *down* position. Hold a treat on the floor in front of him, about 2 inches (5 cm) out of his reach.
2. If your dog makes any attempt to crawl one or two steps to get the treat, issue a *yes!* and reward him. If he keeps standing up during this exercise or shows any sign of frustration, you may be holding the treat too far out of his reach. Try holding it in your closed hand up to his nose, and then draw it slowly away from him until he stretches out to get it. Issue a *yes!* and reward him.
3. When your dog is comfortable with this, start moving the treat a little farther away from him until he takes one or two crawling steps toward it. Again, issue a *yes!* and reward him for his progress. In this way, you can gradually increase the distance you

expect him to crawl. You can begin to use the *crawl* command when he has learned to advance several steps.

# DANCE

## Description

The dog stands on his hind legs and spins around.

## Uses

This trick is cute all by itself, but it can also become part of a canine musical freestyle routine.

## Prerequisites

None.

The *dance* command asks your dog to stand on his hind legs and spin around.

## Training Technique

Some dogs are natural dancers, while others find it more difficult to stand or balance on their hind legs. Physical conformation, especially with long-backed breeds, may make it injurious to practice this skill. Keep these things in mind when choosing which tricks to pursue. If your dog shows reluctance to stand on his hind legs, it may be best to pass on this one.

1. Hold a treat above your dog's head and encourage him to get it. Hold it just high enough so that he has to stand on his hind legs to retrieve it without jumping up. If he stands for the treat, issue a *yes!* and reward him. See if you can get him to stand for several seconds before rewarding him—it will help him develop good balancing skills.

2. When your dog seems comfortable standing on two legs, use the treat to lure him into a circle. Keep the treat close to his nose to encourage him to remain standing as he turns. If necessary, practice turning in smaller increments, beginning with a half turn, then a three-quarter turn, and finally, a full turn. Don't forget to issue a *yes!* and a reward for each measure of success.

3. When your dog has succeeded in making a full turn on his hind legs, begin to use the *dance* command to instruct him what to do. Then slowly begin to fade your treat-luring movements into a less conspicuous hand signal, perhaps a circular motion with your finger.

4. Variation: Your friends will be amazed at your performing pup's talents, but if you really want to turn your Fido into Fred Astaire, hold his paw while he turns, as if you were spinning him. The training technique is the same as the above, except you need to hold his paw with one hand while holding a treat above his head in the other hand as you teach him to turn. Dogs who are not fond of standing on their hind legs may prefer this version of the trick because their human dance partner can help provide balance and stability as they turn. For either version of *dance*, there is always room for human participation. Try doing a spin yourself in sequence with or alternately to your dog's spin. Dancing is, after all, more fun with a partner!

# FACE (ALSO: SALUTE, HIDE)

## Description
The dog puts his paw against his muzzle.

## Uses
This trick is especially entertaining if your dog salutes when you say, "Attention!" or if your dog hides when you say, "The dog catcher is coming!"

## Prerequisites
*Sit*, *stay*, and *shake*.

## Training Technique
1. Hold your hand against the side of your dog's muzzle, or across the top of it, and tell him *shake*.

2. If your dog lifts his paw up to his face to give you a *shake*, tell him *yes!* and reward him.

3. As you practice getting your dog to perform *shake* with your hand against his face, begin to withdraw your hand just as he lifts his paw up. If he touches his face with it, tell him *yes!* and reward him.

4. Eventually, your dog will understand that you want him to touch his face, and then you can begin to ask him to hold his paw

When performing the *face* command, the dog puts his paws against his muzzle.

against it for a few seconds using the *stay* command.

5. When your dog performs *face* to your satisfaction, start using the command (or whatever cue phrase you desire) to name the behavior.

# HIGH FIVE

## Description
The dog raises a paw to give his handler a high five.

## Uses
This trick can provide entertainment for your guests, but it can also be a fun skill for a therapy dog to share with children or the elderly.

## Prerequisites
*Shake.*

## Training Technique
The high five command is easy to teach a dog who already knows how to lift a paw for *shake*. If your dog does not know the *shake* command, teach him this first, then go on to the following steps.

1. Practice *shake* until your dog automatically lifts a paw when you hold out your hand (without giving him the verbal *shake* command). Issue a *yes!* and reward him with a treat each time he performs *shake* when you hold it out.

2. Gradually start holding your hand out at a higher level, and encourage your dog to keep reaching up to touch it with his paw. Issue a *yes!* and reward him each time he touches it.

3. Eventually, you can begin to hold your hand up high with your palm facing your dog, and he will continue to touch your hand with his paw. At this point, you can begin to use the *high five* command so that he associates it with the trick.

## KISS

### Description
The dog licks a person's cheek.

### Uses
Besides being a cute trick to show your friends, *kiss* is also a bonding behavior, as dogs lick each other socially all the time.

### Prerequisites
None.

### Training Technique
Be aware that dogs can harbor bacteria in their mouths, especially after eating raw food, ingesting wild animal carcasses, or raiding the kitty litter box. Some experts do not recommend allowing a dog to kiss you on the face, advice that may be especially important for elderly or immunocompromised individuals. Realistically, the chances of suffering ill effects from engaging in smoochy face with your dog are quite low. Even if you prefer not to take a

*High five* can provide entertainment for your guests, but it can also be a good skill for a therapy dog to share with children or the elderly.

chance with oral contamination, it doesn't mean you have to forego this intimate trick—just teach your dog to kiss your hand instead!

1. Dogs who are heavy lickers generally don't need much prodding to get them to lick a cheek or hand. For these dogs, consistent use of the *kiss* command every time they engage in licking is enough for them to learn its meaning and begin kissing on command.

2. If your dog does not have a very active tongue, he can learn to enjoy kissing if you rub butter on your cheek or hand for him to lick off. Give the *kiss* command and present the buttered area for him to lick. Repetition will

teach him to give you a *kiss* on command whenever you point to your cheek or hand. When he responds reliably, you can stop slathering yourself with condiments.

## OPEN THE DOOR (ALSO: OPEN)

### Description
The dog opens a door on command.

### Uses
This is more than an amusing or useful trick; it is also a skill that assistance dogs

Besides being a cute trick to show your friends, *kiss* encourages bonding behavior because dogs lick each other socially all the time.

often learn. Teach it to your dog if you want his assistance around the house. This trick can become part of a more complicated sequence of behaviors, such as opening a door to fetch a laundry basket. It only works for dogs who are tall enough to reach a door latch.

### Prerequisites
None.

### Training Technique
Be aware that when you teach your dog to open doors, it may become difficult to keep him out of certain areas. If you are afraid he will get into the garbage, pet

food, or other things you normally keep behind closed doors, you may want to pass on this trick.

The easiest type of door latch for a dog to open is a handle latch, so these instructions will focus on teaching *open the door* with this type of mechanism. You may very well decide to install this type of door latch only on certain doors so that you can control your dog's access to specific areas of your home.

## Pushing Open

1. Encourage your dog to jump up on the door latch by holding a treat by it. If he touches it at all with a paw, issue a *yes!* and reward him with the treat.
2. When your dog has no qualms about jumping up on the door and appears to touch the latch consistently, ask him for a little more by teasing him with the treat or holding it right behind the door latch to encourage him to paw at it. When he does, issue a *yes!* and reward him.
3. While practicing this, your dog may trigger the latch and open the door. If he does, profuse praise, in addition to an enthusiastic *yes!* and a food reward, should be lavished upon him! If he does not, encourage him to be more aggressive with his pawing until he can get the door open. When he is able to open it, begin to use the *open the door* command so that he can associate it with the behavior.
4. To proof this behavior, try putting a treat on the other side of the door and give the *open the door* command. He'll

soon learn that a reward awaits him whenever he accomplishes this task.

## Pulling Open

1. Your dog will use a tug rope or rag to pull the door open, so first make sure he will tug on the rope or rag by teasing him with it and playing with it.
2. Next, tie the rope or rag to the end of the door latch, and tease your dog with it to encourage him to pull on it. When he does, issue a *yes!* and reward him with a treat.
3. If your dog pulls hard enough to open the door, profusely praise him, say *yes!* enthusiastically, and give a food reward. If he does not, encourage him to pull harder until he can get the door open. When he succeeds, begin to use

the *open the door* command so that he can associate it with this behavior.

4. To proof *open the door*, try putting a treat on the other side of the door and give the *open the door* command. Your dog will become quite proficient at opening the door when he knows a treat is waiting for him on the other side of it.

## PLAY DEAD (ALSO: BANG)

### Description
The dog lies on his side as if he is dead.

### Uses
This trick can be used as part of a

**Play dead is an easy trick for your dog to learn, and it's always a crowd-pleaser!**

canine musical freestyle routine. You can also use it to access your dog's underside for grooming.

## Prerequisites
*Down* and *stay*.

## Training Technique
It is easier to teach your dog this trick before he learns *roll over* (in this chapter). Once he learns the *roll over* command, it may be difficult to keep him from rolling all the way over when you want him to perform *play dead*.

1. Start with your dog in a *down* position. Hold a treat in front of him to get his attention.
2. Move the treat slowly to your dog's side, keeping him focused on it until he is looking behind him.
3. Next, begin to move the treat slowly over your dog's back. If he flops onto his side in an effort to keep his eyes on the treat, issue a *yes!* and reward him. If he does not, try luring him with the treat a little more slowly until he does. If necessary, break the behavior into smaller segments and begin rewarding him when you get him to look behind him. Then progress to drawing the treat over his back.
4. When you can get your dog to roll onto his side, work on perfecting the trick. As soon as he rolls onto his side, immediately bring the treat in front of him so that he lays his head on the floor, too. If he does what you want, issue a *yes!* and reward him.
5. When your dog has gotten this far with the behavior, begin to use the *play*

*dead* or *bang* command.

6. The final step is to ask your dog to stay when he's in the *play dead* position. Teach him to hold this position until you release him with an *okay*. With practice, he will automatically hold this position without a *stay* command. He'll wait for you to release him.

# RING THE BELL

## Description
The dog pulls on a bell ribbon or bell rope, which is usually attached to a doorknob or handle.

## Uses
This is a handy trick to teach your dog if you'd like him to ring a bell whenever he wants to go outside.

## Prerequisites
*Pull.*

## Training Technique
After teaching your dog the *pull* command from Chapter 11, teach him the more specific *ring the bell* command.

1. Tie the bell ribbon or rope to the handle on the door you normally use to let your dog outside.
2. Tease your dog with the bell ribbon, and give the *pull* command to encourage him to tug on it. When he does, immediately let him outside— this is his reward!
3. When your dog pulls on the bell ribbon willingly, replace the *pull* command with *ring the bell* so that he

learns the specific command for this behavior.

4. Require your dog to ring the bell before each time you let him outside. You can use this command along with *outside* to ask him if he needs to go out, and then tell him to ring the bell before you open the door.

5. Start increasing your distance from the door when you tell your dog to ring the bell. This will help him feel comfortable going up to the bell ribbon on his own to ring it. During this process, he may begin to do this of his own accord whenever he wants to go outside.

## ROLL OVER

### Description
The dog lies on his side and then rolls over onto his other side on command.

### Uses
Getting your dog to roll over is obviously a fun trick, but it can also be part of a canine musical freestyle routine.

### Prerequisites
*Down.*

### Training Technique
If you are interested in teaching your dog *play dead* or *belly up* from Chapter 8, it is best to teach these skills prior to teaching *roll over*. Once he has learned to roll over, it can be difficult to keep him from rolling all the way over when you want to teach him these other two skills.

1. With your dog lying down, show him a treat and draw it toward his side until he is looking behind him.

For *roll over*, the dog lies on his side and then rolls over onto his other side on command.

### Uses

This is an entertaining trick that also works well in canine musical freestyle routines.

### Prerequisites

*Down.*

### Training Technique

If your dog doesn't seem to catch on to this trick with the following training techniques, consider teaching him *back* first (in Chapter 10) so that he can find his reverse gear.

1. With your dog in a *down* position in front of you, shuffle your feet toward him in an effort to crowd him into backing up. Also try waving your hands as if you are shooing away a fly to encourage him to back up.
2. If your dog shows any slight indication of backing up, issue a *yes!* and reward him.
3. Gradually ask your dog to back up a little farther before saying *yes!* and rewarding him. When he consistently scooches backward on his belly, start using the *scooch* command before encouraging him to back up.
4. After your dog has learned to perform this skill to your satisfaction, begin to minimize the physical encouragement you give him and just use the *scooch* command instead. You may also reduce your hand waves into a more subtle hand signal for this trick, like a flick of your wrist.

2. Then slowly begin to draw the treat up and over your dog's back. If he rolls onto his side in an attempt to keep his eyes on the treat, issue a *yes!* and reward him for his progress.
3. Gradually require your dog to roll a little farther before rewarding him.
4. Eventually, you will be able to draw the treat completely over your dog's body to get him to do a full *roll over.*
5. At this point, begin to use the *roll over* command so that your dog associates it with this behavior.
6. Begin using your finger rather than a treat to lure your dog into the *roll over* position, but be sure to keep telling him *yes!* and rewarding him for the trick. You can gradually adapt this hand movement into a more subtle hand signal, such as making a small semicircle in the air with your finger.

## SCOOCH

### Description

The dog crawls backward on command.

## SHAKE

### Description

The dog lifts his paw to shake hands.

## Uses

It may seem like a simple trick, but *shake* has many more uses than it appears on the surface. Use it when trimming your dog's nails. Use it to wipe his feet when he comes in from outside. Use it to assist you in teaching him other tricks that require him to lift a foot, like *face* or *high five*.

## Prerequisites

*Sit*.

## Training Technique

1. Tell your dog to perform *sit* in front of you. Then use your right hand to encourage him to lift his right foot. You can tickle the back of his leg just above his foot, or you can prod the back of his leg with your fingers until he lifts his foot.

2. When your dog lifts his right foot, snatch it up quickly with your right hand and issue a *yes!* Then give him a treat.

> It may seem like a simple trick, but *shake* has many more uses than you may think— use it whenever you need your dog to lift his foot.

3. After a few repetitions, your dog should begin to lift his paw when you hold out your hand. Then you can start giving the *shake* command as you hold out your hand so he can connect this command to his newly learned behavior.

## SPEAK (ALSO: WHAT?)

### Description

The dog barks on command.

## Uses

This is a fun trick you can use to get your dog to bark at amusing times or to create a conversation routine with him. Some people find that teaching their dog to bark on command helps them control inappropriate barking. You can also use this command to spur your dog into giving a barking alarm or to scare intruders away.

## Prerequisites

None.

## Training Technique

This trick can be even more amusing if you teach your dog to bark on a cue other than *speak*, such as *what?* If your dog happens to have a bark that sounds like "mama," you can teach him to bark on the cue, "Who do you love?" If his bark sounds like "oh, no," you can teach him to bark at the cue, "The dogcatcher is coming!"

If you plan to teach your dog to bark at more than one cue so that you can create a conversation routine, teach him to bark for the *speak* command first. Then it will be easy to let him know when he's supposed to bark during the routine.

1. Dogs tend to be very reactive to the barks of other dogs. When one dog in the neighborhood starts barking, you can hear the cacophony spread throughout the neighborhood as the others join in. With this in mind, it should be fairly easy to get your dog to bark if you bark at him. Bark at your dog excitedly to encourage him to join in the barking. When he does, issue a *yes!* and reward him.

### Speak Up—or Not

Some dogs are obviously more vocally communicative than others. Work with your dog's natural talents, and don't expect him to put a lot of enthusiasm into learning the *speak* command if he isn't much of a barker to begin with. Most dogs, however, can learn to give at least a whine or groan to it.

2. When you can get your dog to respond to your barking, begin giving the *speak* command (or other cue command) before encouraging him to bark. Say it sharply so that it simulates (sort of) a bark. Issue a *yes!* and reward him each time he responds by barking.

3. If you desire, you can also teach your dog to bark to a signal, such as holding a hand up to your ear as if you are listening for something. Simply hold your hand to your ear as you tell him *speak*, and eventually he will respond to the hand signal alone.

## SPIN/TURN

### Description

The dog turns in a circle on command.

### Uses

Spinning is a nice trick and a common maneuver in the sport of canine musical freestyle, but it also has other uses. The *spin* command is a good way to get your dog to wipe his own feet when he comes in from the outdoors. You can also use *spin* to help him get his leash or tie out untangled.

## Prerequisites
None.

## Training Technique
When you teach your dog the *spin* command, instruct him to spin in the same direction every time (either clockwise or counterclockwise). If you also want to teach him to spin in the other direction, teach him one direction first and then teach him the other direction using a different command, like *turn*. This way, if you use these commands to untangle your dog, you can tell him exactly which direction to spin.

The *spin* command is a good way to get your dog to wipe his own feet when he comes in from the outdoors.

1. Give your dog the *spin* command, and lure him around in a circle with a treat.
2. When your dog completes the circle, issue a *yes!* and reward him.
3. As your dog gets better at spinning, you can begin to use your finger, instead of a treat, to lure him into performing a circle. Continue to say *yes!* and reward him when he completes it.
4. Begin to minimize your movement until your dog will spin when you make a small circle in the air with your finger. This will be your hand signal for *spin*.
5. To teach your dog *turn*, make sure he is very well versed in *spin* first. Then go through these same steps to teach him to spin in the opposite direction.

## STICK 'EM UP

### Description
The dog sits up and puts his paws in the air when the handler points a finger at him and says, "Stick 'em up."

### Uses
This trick is a variation of beg, but it offers a little more entertainment value.

### Prerequisites
*Sit* and *beg*.

### Training Technique
This trick does require a bit of natural talent. It works best with dogs who tend to lift their paws high for the *beg* position.

1. With your dog in a *sit*, lure him into a *beg* position by holding a treat above his head, just behind his eyes and barely out of his reach. (You may have to hold

it in a closed hand to prevent him from snatching it.)

2. When your dog lifts his front feet off the ground in an attempt to reach the treat, issue a *yes!* and let him have the reward. If he tries to jump up to get it, you may be holding it too high.

3. Gradually require your dog to maintain a *beg* position for a few seconds longer before issuing a *yes!* and allowing him to have the treat. Also, try to encourage him to raise his paws as high as possible by exciting him with the treat or tapping on his paws.

4. When your dog has learned to beg with his paws up, start giving him the *stick 'em up* command when you want him to do this trick. You can also begin to hold your hand like a gun (thumb up and index finger pointed at him) instead of luring him with a treat. Continue to reinforce the behavior with a *yes!* and a reward when he performs the behavior reliably.

## TOUCH (ALSO: NUZZLE)

### Description
The dog nuzzles the hand of a person his handler points out.

### Uses
This trick can be a nice way for your dog to greet people. It is also a great way for therapy dogs to break the ice with anyone who is withdrawn.

### Prerequisites
None.

### Training Technique
Teaching this trick requires the assistance of another person.

1. Have your assistant sit on a couch or chair with her hand resting on her leg. Put a treat under her hand, and give the *touch* command as you encourage your dog to try to get it.

2. If your dog nuzzles the assistant's hand to get the treat, issue a *yes!* The assistant should then immediately lift her hand so that he can have it.

3. Practice Steps 1 and 2 until your dog willingly nuzzles the assistant's hand whenever you issue a *touch*. Try this exercise with the assistant's hand in other positions, such as on the arm of the chair or the end of the couch.

4. When your dog understands what you expect of him when you tell him *touch*, stop putting a treat under the assistant's hand and simply give the *touch* command and point to the hand you want him to nuzzle. Continue to issue a *yes!* and reward him when he performs correctly.

5. Finally, try this trick on other people in other settings by pointing to a person and telling your dog *touch*.

## WAVE (ALSO: WAVE HI, WAVE BYE)

### Description
The dog lifts his paw like he's waving.

### Uses
*Wave* is a fun way for your dog to greet or say goodbye to your friends. It is also an endearing trick for a therapy dog to learn.

## Prerequisites
*High five.*

## Training Technique
1. First, teach your dog the *high five* command in this chapter.
2. Hold your hand out to your dog to perform a *high five*, but when he tries to touch it, pull it away and don't let him touch it.
3. Issue a *yes!* and reward your dog.
4. Practice Steps 2 and 3 until your dog willingly lifts his paw in the air without touching your hand. When he does this, you can start using the *wave* command. (Note that *wave hi* and *wave bye* sound so much alike that you can use them interchangeably.)
5. Begin to hold your hand farther away from your dog when you give the wave command. Gradually transition your *high five* hand motion into a wave so that he learns to wave back at you when you wave to him!

# WEAVE

## Description
The dog weaves back and forth between his handler's legs.

## Uses
This canine musical freestyle maneuver makes an impressive trick, but you can also use it to untangle your dog's leash from around your legs, or use it in place of *switch* to get him from your right side to your left side or vice versa.

## Prerequisites
None.

## Training Technique
It may help to first train your dog in *heel* and *foos* from Chapter 7, especially if you have trouble getting him in a good position for weaving. Also, be sure to start the *weave* by stepping with the leg that is farthest from your dog (i.e., if your dog is on your left side, step with your right foot). Also, teach your dog to pass completely through your legs—this will help you avoid having to step over him, and it makes for a much smoother maneuver.

1. With your dog in a *heel* position on your left side, take a step forward with your right foot.
2. Give the *weave* command, and lure your dog between your legs with a treat in your right hand. (Hold the treat behind your right thigh.)
3. When your dog comes all the way through your legs, issue a *yes!* and reward him.
4. Take a step forward with your left foot.
5. Give the *weave* command, and lure your dog between your legs with a treat in your left hand. (Hold the treat behind your left thigh.)
6. When your dog comes all the way through your legs, issue a *yes!* and reward him.
7. Repeat Steps 1 through 6 until your dog learns how to perform *weave* well. Then you can begin to transition your luring motions into a more subtle waving hand signal, or you can gradually fade your luring motions completely until he responds to the verbal *weave* command alone.

# GLOSSARY OF CANINE TERMINOLOGY

**agility:** A fast-paced interactive sport that mainly consists of multiple obstacles on a timed course that the dog must negotiate at the direction of a handler. Different classes have varying levels of difficulty.

**albino:** A rare congenital condition that results in the lack of pigmentation in the skin, hair, and irises of the eyes

**almond eye:** An eye that is noticeably pointed at either corner and that is oval in shape

**American Kennel Club (AKC):** The official registry for purebred dogs in the United States. Publishes and maintains the Stud Book and handles all litter and individual registrations, transfers of ownership, and so on. Keeps all United States dog show, field trial, and obedience trial records; issues championships and other titles in these areas as they are earned; approves and licenses dog show, obedience trial, and field trial judges; licenses or issues approval to all championship shows, obedience trials, and recognized match shows. Creates and enforces the rules, regulations, and policies by which the breeding, raising, exhibiting, handling, and judging of purebred dogs in the United States are governed. Clubs, not individuals, are members of the American Kennel Club, each of which is represented by a delegate selected from the club's own membership for the purpose of attending the quarterly American Kennel Club meetings as the representative of the member club, to vote on matters discussed at each meeting and to bring back a report to the individual club of any decisions or developments that took place there.

**American Rare Breed Association (ARBA):** The American Rare Breed Association (ARBA) was founded in 1991 to provide information and education about the many breeds of dogs that are not yet recognized by the American Kennel Club (AKC) and are thus considered "rare."

**angulation:** The angles formed by the meeting of the bones, generally referring to the shoulder and upper arm in the forequarters and the stifle and hock in the hindquarters

**ankle joint:** See hock

**apron:** The long hair that extends from the mane into the sides and under the neck and on the front of the chest. Also known as the bib or ruff (q.v.).

**Australian National Kennel Council (ANKC):** The Australian National Kennel Council (ANKC), which held its first meeting in 1949, serves as the administrative body for pure breed canine affairs in Australia but does not deal directly with breeders, exhibitors, or judges. These affairs are governed by branches in the individual territories.

**back:** The portion of the topline (dorsal surface) that begins just behind the withers and ends at the loins/croup; technically, the lumbar and thoracic regions of the spine.

**backline:** The entire topline from the rear end of the withers to the tip of the tail

**balance:** Symmetry and proportion. A well-balanced dog is one in which all of the parts appear in correct ratio to one another: height to length, head to body, skull to foreface (muzzle), and neck to head and body.

**bat ear:** An erect ear, relatively broad at the base and rounded at the top, opening directly to the front

**beard:** Long, thick hair growth on the muzzle, especially on the lower jaw

**benched show:** A show where dogs are judged on their appearance. Although most modern shows allow the exhibitor to show her dog and then leave, in the past the dogs were put on display on a bench all day for spectators. Thus, the term "benched showing" has remained as a general synonym for conformation showing.

**Best in Show:** The dog or bitch chosen as the most representative of any dog in any breed from among the group winners at an all-breed dog show. (The dog or bitch who has won Best of Breed next competes in the group of which its breed is a part. Then the first-prize winner of each group meets in an additional competition from which one is selected the Best in Show winner.)

**bicolor:** Two-colored coats, usually of sharply contrasting colors

**bitch:** A female dog

**bite:** The manner in which the upper and lower jaws meet

**Blenheim:** A chestnut (red-brown) and white coat color pattern (e.g., Cavalier King Charles Spaniel). The chestnut markings are on a pearly white background, and the color must cover both ears and eyes, with a white blaze between the ears and eyes.

**blood trailing:** The act of a dog following a trail of blood from a wounded animal, even when the trail has been there for a few hours

**bobtail:** A tailless dog or one whose tail has been docked very short

**bone:** Quality, strength, and substance of leg bones in proportion to the overall size of the dog. A dog called "good in bone" has legs that are correct in girth for his breed and for his own general conformation.

**breed:** A race of domestic purebred dogs descended from mutual ancestors (having a common gene pool), refined and developed by man

**breeder:** A person who breeds dogs

**breed standard:** The official description of the ideal specimen of a breed. The Standard of Perfection is drawn up by the parent specialty club (usually by a special committee to whom the task is assigned), is approved by the membership, and then serves as a guide to breeders and to judges in decisions regarding the merit, or lack of it, in evaluating individual dogs.

**brindle:** A tiger-striped coat pattern, usually a mixture of black with brown, tan, or gold. Darker hairs in the coat form bands and produce a striping effect on a background of lighter-colored hairs.

**brisket:** The part of the body between the forelegs and beneath the chest

**broken coat:** A crinkly, rough wire coat, most often applied to terriers. It comprises a harsh outercoat and a dense, soft undercoat. See wire coat.

**broken color:** A solid-colored coat that is interrupted by patches of a different color, usually white with darker colors. See particolor (q.v.), piebald (q.v.), pied (q.v.).

**Canadian Kennel Club (CKC):** The principle dog registry in Canada. Formed in 1887, the organization devoted itself to the promotion of breeding and exhibiting "thoroughbred" dogs in Canada, the formulation of rules for the governing of dog exhibition, as well as the recommendation of able judges and the official opening of a registry for purebred dogs.

**canine freestyle:** A competitive sport that combines obedience and dance to display teamwork and rapport between dog and handler

**canines:** Dogs, jackals, wolves, and foxes as a group. Also the two upper and lower long, pointed teeth (fangs) separated within each jaw by the incisors.

**carpals:** On the front leg, the joint connecting the forearm and the pastern

**carting:** A competitive sport in which the dog pulls a handler in a three- or four-wheel cart with a seat. The emphasis is not on how much weight the dog can pull but on handler control and the dog's ability to maneuver the cart.

**cat foot:** A short-toed, round, tight foot similar to that of a cat

**Challenge Certificate:** A card awarded at dog shows in Great Britain by which championship there is gained. Comparable to Winners Dog and Winners Bitch awards in the United States. To become a British champion, a dog must win three of these Challenge Certificates at designated championship dog shows.

**chamois cloth:** A grooming tool used to polish and shine the coats of shorthaired dogs

**Champion:** A dog or bitch who has won a total of 15 points, including two majors, the total number under not less than three judges, two of whom must have awarded the majors at AKC point shows.

**character:** Appearance, behavior, and temperament considered correct in an individual breed of dog

**cheeky:** Cheeks that bulge out or are rounded in appearance

**chest:** The part of the body enclosed by the ribs

**chiseled:** Clean-cut below the eyes

**chop mouth:** A hound who does not have a long, drawn-out bay but more of a short, choppy bark as he follows the scent trail

**chops:** Pendulous, loose skin creating jowls. See flews.

**close coupled:** Compact in appearance; short in the loin.

**close trailing:** Following a scent trail silently

**cobby:** Short bodied; compact.

**coat:** The hair that covers a dog's body

**cold nosed:** Refers to a hound who is capable of following a "cold" scent, i.e., one that is either old and/or one that is difficult to find and follow

**cold trailer:** Refers to a hound, usually slow working, who has the inherent ability of nose as well as the desire, endurance, and tenacity to follow a cold trail, one that is either old and/or difficult to find and follow

**condition:** General fitness and health. A dog said to be in good condition is one carrying exactly the right amount of weight, whose coat looks alive and glossy, and who exhibits a general appearance and demeanor of well-being.

**conformation:** The framework of the dog; his form and structure. In show ring competition, conformation denotes the overall quality of a dog's structure, form, and arrangement of the parts in conformance to the breed standard.

**couching:** An archaic term describing the action of hunting dogs who, when scenting game, slowly crept nearer while lowering themselves to the ground. This was a trait desired when birds were captured with nets or when the dog found birds for the falcon.

**corded coat:** Natural interweaving of the outercoat and undercoat, forming individual long, tight curls or cords, similar to dreadlocks. Corded coats are virtually waterproof.

**coupling:** The section of the body known as the loin (between the ribs and hindquarters). A short-coupled dog is one in whom the loin is short.

**crest:** The uppermost arched portion of the back of the neck, from the nape to the beginning of the withers.

**crop:** To cut the ear leather, usually to cause the ear to stand erect. This practice is banned in some parts of the world.

**croup:** The portion of the back directly above the hind legs

**crown:** The top part of the head; dome of the topskull

**curly coat:** Short, tight, full curls. This coat type provides protection from the elements and water.

**cynology:** The study of canines

**dam:** Female parent of a dog or bitch

**dapple:** Mottling or spotting on the coat; unpatterned and irregular darker patches on a lighter-colored background.

**dentition:** Arrangement of the teeth

**dewclaw:** An extra claw or functionless digit on the inside of the leg. Dewclaws are generally removed several days following a puppy's birth. Required in some breeds, unimportant in others, and sometimes a disqualification—all according to the individual breed standard.

**dewlap:** Excess loose and pendulous skin under the throat and neck

**dish faced:** The tip of the nose is placed higher than the stop

**disqualification:** A fault or condition that renders a dog ineligible to compete in organized shows, designated by the breed standard or by a leading dog registry

**dock:** To shorten the tail by cutting it. This practice is banned in some parts of the world.

**dock diving:** A competitive sport in which dogs race down a dock, then jump off the end and into the water, with distance being the goal

**dog:** A male of the species. Also used to describe male and female canines collectively.

**dog show:** A competition in which dogs have been entered for the purpose of evaluation and to receive the opinion of a judge

**domed:** A topskull that is rounded rather than flat

**double coat:** A dog's usual coat, consisting of a protective outercoat and an undercoat that provides warmth

**down faced:** A downward inclination of the muzzle toward the tip of the nose

**drag:** A trail having been prepared by dragging a bag, generally bearing the strong scent of an animal, along the ground. Also the trail left by an animal in transit.

**drive:** Powerful hindquarter propulsion denoting sound locomotion

**drop ear:** Ears carried drooping or folded forward

**dry head:** A head exhibiting no excess wrinkling

**dry neck:** A clean, firm neckline free of throatiness or excess skin

**dual champion:** A dog who has won both bench show and field trial championships

**earthdog:** A sporting event that tests a dog's instincts and ability to work underground in search of quarry in timed courses designed to simulate hunting conditions. Some courses consist of actual underground tunnels, while others consist of artificially constructed aboveground passages.

**elbow:** The joint of the forearm and upper arm

**erect ear:** An upright or prick ear that is either blunt or pointed and tipped

**even bite:** Exact meeting of the front teeth, tip to tip, with no overlap of the uppers or lowers. Generally considered to be less serviceable than the scissors bite, although equally permissible or preferred in some breeds. Also known as a level bite.

**expression:** The typical expression of the breed as one studies the head. Determined largely by the shape of the eye and its placement.

**fancier:** A person actively involved in the sport of purebred dogs

**fancy:** The enthusiasts of a sport or hobby. Dog breeders, exhibitors, judges, and others actively involved with purebred dogs as a group compose the dog fancy.

**feathering:** The longer fringes of hair that appear on the ears, tail, chest, and legs

**Fédération Cynologique Internationale (FCI):** A canine authority representing numerous countries, principally European, all of which consent to and agree on certain practices and breed identifications. Recognizing each breed of the countries it includes, the FCI registers hundreds of breeds—each of the breeds that are federated are eligible for the International Championship.

**fetch:** Retrieving of game by a dog. Also the command for a dog to do so.

**fetlock:** An excessively sloping pastern

**field champion:** A dog who has defeated a specified number of dogs in specified competitions at a series of American Kennel Club (AKC) licensed or member field trials

**field trial:** A competition for specified hound or sporting breeds where dogs are judged according to their ability and style on following a game trail or on finding and retrieving game

**filled-up face:** Smooth, cleanly muscled facial contours

**finishing a dog:** Completing a dog's championship, obedience title, or field trial title

**flag:** Feathering on the tail. Also a long tail carried high.

**flank:** The side of the body between the last rib and the hip

**flat bone:** Bones of the leg that are not round

**flat sided:** Ribs that are flat down the side rather than slightly rounded

**flews:** Pendulous skin that hangs from the muzzle at the corners of the mouth

**flop ear:** An ear that fails to remain erect, not to be confused with a drop ear, which is naturally pendant

**flush:** To drive birds from cover, to spring at them, to force them to take flight

**flyball:** A competitive sporting event that involves relay races in which several teams of dogs compete against each other and the clock, jumping over hurdles to retrieve a ball released into the air

**flying disc:** A sporting event where the dog races into the ring to leap and snatch a disc thrown high into the air and return it to the handler at the starting position. A time is set, and scoring depends upon the number of catches, distance, accuracy, and artistry of the dog within that time limit.

**flying ear:** An ear correctly carried, dropped, or folded that stands up or tends to fly upon occasion

**fold ear:** A drop ear that hangs in a fold rather than remaining flat to the head

**forearm:** Lower part of the forelimb. The region below the elbow and the wrist.

**foreface:** The muzzle of the dog

**forequarters:** The dog's front assembly, from the shoulder blade down to the feet

**Foundation Stock Service®:** A record-keeping service provided by the American Kennel Club (AKC) to document rare purebred dogs. They are not eligible for AKC registration, although breeds that meet certain criteria are permitted to participate in companion events.

**front:** The forepart of the body viewed head-on. Includes the head, forelegs, shoulders, chest, and feet.

**fringe:** Long hair that drapes over the ears, covers the tail, or supplements the chest and belly

**furnishings:** Long hair on the extremities, including the head and tail

**gait:** The manner in which a dog walks or trots

**gallop:** The fastest gait. Never to be used in the show ring but often used when hunting, racing, etc.

**game:** Animals or wild birds that are hunted

**guard hairs:** The longest coarse hairs that grow through the outercoat to cover and protect the undercoat. They are usually water repellant.

**gay tail:** A tail carried high

**gazehound:** A general name for the swift hounds who run by sight; a synonym for sighthound or windhound.

**girth:** Measurement of the chest circumference taken behind the withers at the point of maximum development

**give tongue:** This phrase is used as a synonym for bay, howl, or open—all terms meaning that the dog is vocal when he is following a scent trail

**groom:** To bathe, brush, comb, and trim a dog; also includes nail and dental care.

**groups:** Refers to the variety groups in which all dog breeds are divided

**gundog:** A dog who has been specifically trained to work with a human in the field for retrieving game that has been shot and for locating live game.

**guns:** The persons who do the shooting during field trials

**gun shy:** Describes a dog who cringes or shows other signs of fear at the sound or sight of a gun

**hackney action:** High lifting of the forefeet accompanied by flexing of the wrists in the manner of a hackney pony

**hard mouthed:** A dog who grasps the game too firmly in retrieving, causing bites and tooth marks

**hare foot:** An elongated paw, like the foot of a hare

**harlequin:** Pied color coat pattern of black or blue-gray on a white background. The color patches are usually of like size and appear ragged. See pied.

**haw:** The red membrane (third eyelid) in the inner corner of a dog's eye. When a dog has a lot of heavy facial skin or loose hanging lids, the haw is more apparent.

**herding trial:** A competitive sport in which the dogs move sheep or other flocking animals around a field, fences, gates, or enclosures under commands from their handlers

**hindquarters:** The rear assembly of the dog (pelvis, thighs, hocks, and paws)

**hock:** The joint between the lower thigh and the metatarsus (rear pastern); the dog's true heel.

**hooded ears:** Small ears with forward-curving edges

**hot nosed:** Refers to a dog who can follow a fresh trail, one made by an animal that has an easy-to-follow scent (like a fox)

**hot trailer:** Refers to a hound who follows a hot scent, usually at much greater speed than the cold trailer

**hound glove:** A grooming tool that slips over the hand like a mitt; it is used to polish and shine short coats and remove loose hair

**hunt test:** A performance event designed to test a dog's natural hunting ability and training. Hunt test are noncompetitive, with the goal based on qualifying in various categories rather than winning

**inbreeding:** The practice of mating two closely related dogs of the same breed

**interbreeding:** The practice of mating dogs of different breeds, often to create a new breed

**jowls:** Pendulous or heavy lips

**keel:** The rounded outline of the lower chest from the prosternum to the end of the breastbone

**kennel:** A building in which dogs are housed. Also used when referring to a person's collective dogs.

**Kennel Club (KC):** Founded in 1873, the Kennel Club of Great Britain is the principle dog-registering organization in the country. The registry's objective and purpose is to promote the improvement of dogs, dog shows, field trials, working trials, and obedience tests. Functioning in an advisory capacity to the organization is an elected body of persons with similar objectives to the club, breeding, training, and exhibiting of purebred dogs.

**kneecap:** The stifle, with the bone known as the patella

**layback:** Proper shoulder angulation. Also a short-faced dog whose pushed-in nose placement is accompanied by an undershot jaw.

**leather:** The ear flap; the outer ear supported by cartilage. Also the skin of the actual nose.

**level bite:** A bite in which the teeth of both jaws meet exactly. Also known as an even bite.

**lippy:** Lips that are pendulous or do not fit tightly

**loin:** The area of the sides between the lower ribs and hindquarters

**loose eyed:** Refers to sheepherding dogs who can direct sheep using eye contact (see strong eyed) but can also round them up by heeling; their eye contact is not as intense as that of the strong-eyed dog.

**long coat:** Long coats consist of very long hair that requires frequent grooming to prevent tangling and matting

**lumbering:** A clumsy, awkward gait

**lure coursing:** Originally, a sporting event where sighthounds coursed after live game, although most modern contests use a rag or mechanical lure for the dogs to chase. Scoring is based on speed, agility, endurance, enthusiasm, and follow.

**luxation:** Dislocation of an anatomical structure such as the patella or lens of the eye

**mane:** The long hair growing on the top and upper sides of the neck

**mask:** Dark facial shading that occurs on some breeds

**mate:** To breed a dog and a bitch to one another. Littermates are dogs who are born in the same litter.

**medium coat:** Medium coats are generally longer than 1 inch (2.5 cm). They are easy to groom and do not develop mats, although thick double coats at this length can develop them if not brushed regularly.

**merle:** A color pattern characterized by dark blotches on a lighter background of the same pigments

**Miscellaneous Class (AKC):** A class provided at American Kennel Club (AKC) point shows in which specified breeds may compete in the absence of their own breed classification, until they are officially recognized.

**mouthy:** The quality of a hound who is needlessly noisy. Also a dog who puts everything into his mouth or nips.

**mustache:** Long, thick hair growth on the upper muzzle

**muzzle:** The part of the head in front of the eyes; the forward sections of the jaw. Also to fasten something over the mouth, usually to prevent biting.

**nape:** The region marked by the skull base and top of the neck's junction

**nonslip retriever:** A dog not expected to flush or to find game; one who merely walks at heel, marks the fall, then retrieves upon command.

**nose:** The dog's organ of smell. Also refers to his talent at scenting. A dog with a "good nose" is one adept at picking up and following a scent trail.

**obedience trial:** A licensed obedience trial is one at which a dog must perform a number of obedience commands, ranging from basic to advanced depending upon the event, with the goal being to earn a title

**obedience trial champion:** Denotes that a dog has attained obedience trial championship under by having gained a specified number of points and first place awards

**occiput:** Upper back point of the skull

**open trailing:** When a hound begins baying as soon as he has found the scent (opens) and continues as long as he is on the trail

**outercoat:** The harsh, longer, exterior jacket of a double-coated dog

**overshot:** Incisors of the upper jaw project beyond the incisors of the lower jaw, causing an incorrect bite

**pad:** Thick protective covering of the bottom of the foot that serves as a shock absorber

**parent club:** National club for a breed

**particolor:** A variegated coat pattern with patches of two or more colors. See broken color (q.v.), piebald (q.v.), pied (q.v.).

**pastern:** The region of the foreleg between the wrist and the digits

**patterned white:** White markings restricted to a symmetrical pattern on the feet, tail tip, chest mark, facial blaze, and sometimes a collar; also called Boston or Irish spotting.

**pedigree:** The record of a purebred dog's ancestry. Pedigrees usually include at least three generations of a dog's descent.

**pelvis:** Hip bone

**piebald:** A coat pattern in which a white background is superimposed with large irregular but symmetrically placed black patches. See broken color (q.v.), particolor (q.v.), pied (q.v.).

**pied:** A coat color pattern displaying uneven patches of two or more colors on a white background. See broken color (q.v.), particolor (q.v.), piebald (q.v.)

**pile:** Dense undercoat of soft hair

**plume:** A long fringe of hair on the tail

**police dog:** Any dog who has been trained to do police work

**poll:** Top of the head

**pluck:** To remove dead hair from a dog's coat by hand

**prick ear:** An erect ear, usually pointed at the tip

**Provisional Acceptance (FCI):** Dogs who are provisionally accepted by the Fédération Cynologique Internationale (FCI) are not eligible for the Certificat d' Aptitude au Championnat International de Beauté (CACIB), meaning that they cannot become an FCI International Champion.

**purebred:** A dog whose sire and dam are of the same breed and who are themselves of unmixed descent since recognition of the breed

**quality:** Excellence of type and conformation

**racy:** Lightly built, appearing overly long in leg; clean cut and aerodynamic, displaying a certain elegance.

**rake:** A grooming tool used for brushing and undercoat care. The long teeth deeply penetrate the undercoat to remove tangles, debris, and dead hair without removing the other hair. Useful for breeds with thick, heavy coats and undercoats.

**rally:** A competitive sport drawing on obedience and agility, in which the dog and handler must execute a course consisting of stations at which they must demonstrate specific skills. Courses become more difficult at higher levels of competition. Also known as rally obedience, rally-o.

**rangy:** Excessive length of body combined with shallowness through the ribs and chest

**reach:** The length of the forward stride of the forelegs, which should correspond with the strength and drive of the hindquarters

**register:** To record a dog's breeding information with a breed-registering organization

**retrieve:** To bring back shot game to the handler

**ridge:** Usually refers to an atypical coat growth pattern in which the hair grows lengthwise along the top of the back against the grain of the coat

**roach back:** A convex curvature of the topline of the dog

**roan:** Individual colored hairs in white markings. Red hairs create a "red roan," and black hairs give a steel gray appearance called "blue" or "blue roan."

**rolling gait:** An aimless, ambling type of action correct in some breeds but faulted in others

**rosettes:** Tan patches on the coat on both shoulder fronts common on dogs with a typical black base coloration. Also patches of hair over the loins in a Poodle clip.

**ruff:** Thick, long hair that encircles the entire neck

**rump:** A small area located on the rear dorsal area of the dog between the loin and the buttocks

**saddle:** A black marking on the coat that runs the length of the back, often from the shoulders to the croup or rump, and extends down the sides, suggestive of a saddle

**schutzhund:** A performance event that tests the obedience, tracking, and protection work skills of working dogs. Courses demand stamina, high intelligence, and versatility and become more difficult at higher levels.

**scissors bite:** The outer tips of the lower incisors touch the inner tips of the upper incisors. Generally considered to be the most serviceable type of jaw formation.

**search and rescue:** Search and rescue dogs are

trackers who follow a human scent to locate missing persons using their senses of smell and hearing under all conditions in various environments. One search and rescue dog is equivalent to 20 searchers in a given area.

**selective breeding:** The process by which a breeder cultivates a breed over time by selecting particular qualities within individuals in the breed that would be best to pass on to future generations

**self-colored:** A dog who is a solid color without white markings

**semi-open trailing:** On trail, the dog will bark some of the time but really begins howling when he has the quarry treed (q.v.)

**semi-prick ear:** An ear characterized by a forward-bending tip. Also referred to as a semi-drop ear.

**service dogs:** Also known as mobility dogs, service dogs are trained to assist physically disabled persons in managing everyday activities. They are also trained in safety procedures.

**shanks:** Thigh region

**shelly:** A narrow body lacking in bone

**short coat:** Short coats are the easiest to groom. They are shiny, sleek, and grow close to the skin. Simple brushing is all that is required to keep them maintained.

**shoulder:** The area comprising the shoulder blade and the mass of muscle, tendon, and ligament surrounding it.

**shoulder height:** The height of the dog from the ground to the highest point of the withers

**single coat:** A coat comprising one consistent type of hair without an undercoat

**sire:** The male parent

**skijoring:** A dog sport that combines cross-country skiing and carting, with the handler as a driver. Attached to the handler on a long bungee cord, the dog wears a pulling harness and must respond instantly to voice commands given by the skier during a race.

**sledding:** Competitive sled-dog racing that tests the performance ability of working dogs, especially huskies. The most celebrated race is the Iditarod, which takes 10 to 28 days to complete.

**slicker brush:** A wire pin brush with a hook pin that helps break up mats

**snippy:** A pointed, weak muzzle

**soundness:** Mental and physical stability. Sometimes used to denote the manner in which the dog gaits.

**square body:** A dog whose measurements from the withers to the ground equal that from the withers to the base of the tail

**stack:** To set up a dog in show position for judging

**stance:** Manner of standing

**standoff coat:** A type of double coat consisting of long, harsh hairs that stand out from the body and support a soft undercoat

**station:** The comparative distance from the withers to the point of the elbow versus the distance from the point of the elbow to the ground

**stifle:** The joint of the hind leg corresponding to a person's knee

**stockings:** White markings covering the feet and extending to cover a portion of the legs

**stop:** Located between the eyes, the stop is the slopping down of the skull in this area; the indentation between the eyes where the cranium and nasal bones meet.

**straight behind:** Lacking angulation in the hindquarters

**stripping:** The removal of dead hair from a dog's coat with a stripping knife

**strong eyed:** Refers to sheepherding dogs who have intense qualities of staring down and almost hypnotically directing sheep by eye contact

**stud:** A male dog used for breeding

**studbook:** The official record kept on the breeding particulars of recognized dog breeds

**substance:** Degree of bone size

**symmetry:** Balance and harmony between all parts of the dog, with no one component dominating or detracting

**tail:** The hindmost portion of the dog's anatomy where the caudal vertebrae gradually tapers to a tip. Not all dogs have tails.

**tail set:** The manner in which the tail is placed on the rump

**therapy work:** Therapy dogs are trained to work as comforters and companions to the physically and mentally disabled, as well as to confined and elderly patients who are unable to keep dogs of their own

**thigh:** The hindquarters from the stifle to the hip

**throatiness:** Excessive loose skin under the throat and neck

**ticking:** Small dots of dark color on a white coat pattern, usually typical of hounds and gundogs. Also called speckling and flecking.

**topknot:** A tuft of long, woolly, or silky hair tied on the top of the head

**topline:** The dog's back from withers to tail set

**tracking:** A competitive sporting event designed primarily to test a dog's ability to discriminate scent

**treeing:** The act of chasing an animal up into a tree and holding it there for a hunter to shoot; most often performed by coonhounds

**trail:** To hunt by following a trail scent

**tricolor:** A three-color coat pattern consisting of white, black, and tan

**trim:** To groom a coat by clipping or plucking

**trot:** The gait at which a dog moves in a rhythmic two-beat action, right front and left hind foot and left front and right hind foot each striking the ground together

**trousers:** Longish hair at the back of both upper and lower thighs

**tuck-up:** The amount of waistline behind the rib cage, measured as the depth of body at the loin (shallow body depth at the loin). Most pronounced in sighthounds.

**tulip ear:** An ear that stands upright with slightly forward-curving edges

**type:** The combination of features that makes a breed unique, distinguishing it from all others

**undercoat:** The dense soft, short coat concealed by the longer outercoat

**underline:** The combined contours of the brisket and the abdominal floor

**undershot:** The front teeth of the lower jaw reach beyond the front teeth of the upper jaw, causing an incorrect bite

**United Kennel Club (UKC):** The United Kennel Club (UKC) was established in 1898 by Mr. Chauncey Z. Bennett and is the second-largest all-breed registry in the United States. It is privately owned and controlled. Through its registration system, the UKC offers a six- or seven-generation pedigree to qualifying registrants.

**unsound:** A dog who is incapable, physically or mentally, of performing the functions for which he was bred

**upper arm:** The foreleg between the forearm and the shoulder blade

**vent:** The anus, or the area under the tail

**voice:** The bark or cry of a hound

**walk:** The gait in which three feet support the body, each lifting in regular sequence, one at a time, off the ground

**weediness:** Light and insufficient bone

**weight pulling:** A competitive sport designed to test strength and stamina. To earn titles, a harnessed dog must pull a sled or cart holding a specified weight for a prescribed distance within a set time limit.

**wire coat:** Wire coats are hard, coarse, and wiry. This type of coat requires frequent grooming and stripping to keep the hair harsh and crisp. See broken coat.

**withers:** The highest point of the shoulders, right behind the neck

**zygomatic arch:** The bony ridge that forms the lower part of the eye socket (orbit)

# TRAINING GLOSSARY

**alternative words:** Alternative words are used in place of the main command word entry in order to avoid using commands that sound very similar to previously trained words, which can be confusing to the animal being trained

**bridge:** Covers a gap in training, such as the time gap between a dog's behavior and the delivery of a food reward for that behavior

**basic communication:** Basic communication relies on cue words or commands that help the trainers communicate what they want from a dog

**clicker training:** A method of animal training that uses a handheld clicking device as a bridge between the desired behavior and the delivery of a food reward

**exercise first:** The practice of using exercise to calm a dog down prior to training

**fade/fading:** The process used to gradually eliminate food rewards for a particular skill by rewarding every other performance of that skill, and then every third performance of that skill, and so on, until rewards are completely phased out; it also refers to the transition of luring motions into hand signals

**food reward:** A small treat used as a lure or as an incentive to reward a dog for a desired behavior

**generalization:** Generalization is the ability of a dog to apply his knowledge to new situations without additional training

**lure:** A lure consists of using a treat to entice a dog to move a certain way or adopt a certain position

**negative punishment:** Taking something away from a dog that he wants, like attention or playtime, to discourage an undesirable behavior

**obedience:** Obedience comprises canine skills that allow a handler to have control over a dog's movement and behavior

**piloerection:** When the hair at the peak of a dog's shoulders, and sometimes along the spine of the back, stands on end

**positive training methods:** Positive training methods employ positive incentives for canine compliance rather than compulsory punishments

**power commands:** Power command words reinforce and support the handler's leadership status with a dog

**prerequisite:** Prerequisites consist of skills that a dog must know before he will be able to master a cue or command

**preventives:** Preventive methods make it difficult or impossible for a dog to engage in undesirable behaviors

**proofing:** Proofing is used to strengthen a behavior, usually by practicing it in a more distracting or challenging environment

**recall:** Recall is when a dog responds appropriately to the *come* command

**training devices:** Appliances that can assist in training a dog

**training techniques:** Training techniques consist of instructions on how to teach a dog a particular command word

**verbal pressure:** Verbal prodding that may include repeating words urgently in fast succession or with escalating volume until a dog responds

# RESOURCES

## ASSOCIATIONS AND ORGANIZATIONS

### Breed Clubs

**American Kennel Club (AKC)**
8051 Arco Corporate Drive, Suite 100
Raleigh, NC 27617-3390
Telephone: (919) 233-9767
Fax: (919) 233-3627 \
E-Mail: info@akc.org
www.akc.org

**Canadian Kennel Club (CKC)**
200 Ronson Drive, Suite 400
Etobicoke, Ontario M9W 5Z9
Telephone: (416) 675-5511
Fax: (416) 675-6506
E-Mail: information@ckc.ca
www.ckc.ca

**The Dachshund Club (UK)**
Honorary Secretary: Mrs. Anne Moore
E-Mail: romanchiwires@aol.com
www.dachshundclub.co.uk

**Dachshund Club of America (DCA)**
Corresponding Secretary: Cheryl Shultz
E-Mail: cherevee@sbcglobal.net
www.dachshundclubofamerica.org

**Fédération Cynologique Internationale (FCI)**
FCI Office
Place Albert 1er, 13
B – 6530 Thuin
Belgique
Telephone: +32 71 59.12.38
Fax: +32 71 59.22.29
www.fci.be

The Kennel Club (UK)
1-5 Clarges Street, Piccadilly, London W1J 8AB
Telephone: 0844 463 3980
Fax: 020 7518 1028
www.thekennelclub.org.uk

National Miniature Dachshund Club (NMDC)
Secretary: Aubrey Nash
E-Mail: Aubray@aol.com
www.dachshund-nmdc.org

United Kennel Club (UKC)
100 E. Kilgore Road
Kalamazoo, MI 49002-5584
Telephone: (269) 343-9020
Fax: (269) 343-7037
www.ukcdogs.com

## Pet Sitters

National Association of Professional Pet Sitters (NAPPS)
15000 Commerce Parkway, Suite C
Mt. Laurel, New Jersey 08054
Telephone: (856) 439-0324
Fax: (856) 439-0525
E-Mail: napps@petsitters.org
www.petsitters.org

Pet Sitters International
201 East King Street
King, NC 27021-9161
Telephone: (336) 983-9222
Fax: (336) 983-5266
E-Mail: info@petsit.com
www.petsit.com

## Rescue Organizations and Animal Welfare Groups

American Humane Association
1400 16th Street NW, Suite 360
Washington, DC 20036
Telephone: (800) 227-4645
E-Mail: info@americanhumane.org
www.americanhumane.org

American Society for the Prevention of Cruelty to Animals (ASPCA)
424 E. 92nd Street
New York, NY 10128-6804
Telephone: (212) 876-7700
www.aspca.org

Royal Society for the Prevention of Cruelty to Animals (RSPCA)
RSPCA Advice Team
Wilberforce Way
Southwater
Horsham
West Sussexl
RH13 9RS
United Kingdom
Telephone: 0300 1234 999
www.rspca.org.uk

## Sports

International Agility Link (IAL)
85 Blackwall Road
Chuwar, Queensland
Australia 4306
Telephone: 61 (07) 3202 2361
Fax: 61 (07) 3281 6872
E-Mail: steve@agilityclick.com
www.agilityclick.com/~ial/

The North American Dog Agility Council (NADAC)
24605 Dodds Rd.
Bend, Oregon 97701
www.nadac.com

**North American Flyball Association (NAFA)**
1333 West Devon Avenue, #512
Chicago, IL 60660
Telephone: (800) 318-6312
Fax: (800) 318-6312
E-Mail: flyball@flyball.org
www.flyball.org

**United States Dog Agility Association (USDAA)**
P.O. Box 850955
Richardson, TX 75085
Telephone: (972) 487-2200
Fax: (972) 231-9700
www.usdaa.com

**The World Canine Freestyle Organization, Inc.**
P.O. Box 350122
Brooklyn, NY 11235
Telephone: (718) 332-8336
Fax: (718) 646-2686
E-Mail: WCFODOGS@aol.com
www.worldcaninefreestyle.org

## Therapy

**Pet Partners**
875 124th Ave, NE, Suite 101
Bellevue, WA 98005
Telephone: (425) 679-5500
Fax: (425) 679-5539
E-Mail: info@petpartners.org
www.petpartners.org

**Therapy Dogs Inc.**
P.O. Box 20227
Cheyenne, WY 82003
Telephone: (877) 843-7364
Fax: (307) 638-2079
E-Mail: therapydogsinc@qwestoffice.net
www.therapydogs.com

**Therapy Dogs International (TDI)**
88 Bartley Road
Flanders, NJ 07836
Telephone: (973) 252-9800
Fax: (973) 252-7171
E-Mail: tdi@gti.net
www.tdi-dog.org

## Training

**American College of Veterinary Behaviorists (ACVB)**
College of Veterinary Medicine, 4474 TAMU
Texas A&M University
College Station, Texas 77843-4474
www.dacvb.org

**American Kennel Club Canine Health Foundation, Inc. (CHF)**
P. O. Box 900061
Raleigh, NC 27675
Telephone: (888) 682-9696
Fax: (919) 334-4011
www.akcchf.org

**Association of Professional Dog Trainers (APDT)**
104 South Calhoun Street
Greenville, SC 29601
Telephone: (800) PET-DOGS
Fax: (864) 331-0767
E-Mail: information@apdt.com
www.apdt.com

**International Association of Animal Behavior Consultants (IAABC)**
565 Callery Road
Cranberry Township, PA 16066
E-Mail: info@iaabc.org
www.iaabc.org

National Association of Dog Obedience
Instructors (NADOI)
7910 Picador Drive
Houston, TX 77083-4918
Telephone: (972) 296-1196
E-Mail: info@nadoi.org
www.nadoi.org

## Veterinary and Health Resources

### The Academy of Veterinary Homeopathy (AVH)
P. O. Box 232282
Leucadia, CA 92023-2282
Telephone: (866) 652-1590
Fax: (866) 652-1590
www.theavh.org

### American Academy of Veterinary Acupuncture (AAVA)
P.O. Box 1058
Glastonbury, CT 06033
Telephone: (860) 632-9911
www.aava.org

### American Animal Hospital Association (AAHA)
12575 W. Bayaud Ave.
Lakewood, CO 80228
Telephone: (303) 986-2800
Fax: (303) 986-1700
E-Mail: info@aahanet.org
www.aahanet.org

### American College of Veterinary Internal Medicine (ACVIM)
1997 Wadsworth Blvd., Suite A
Lakewood, CO 80214-5293
Telephone: 303-231-9933
Telephone (US or Canada): (800) 245-9081
Fax: (303) 231-0880
E-Mail: ACVIM@ACVIM.org
www.acvim.org

### American College of Veterinary Ophthalmologists (ACVO)
P.O. Box 1311
Meridian, ID 83860
Telephone: (208) 466-7624
Fax: (208) 466-7693
E-Mail: office13@acvo.com
www.acvo.org

### American Heartworm Society (AHS)
P.O. Box 8266
Wilmington, DE 19803-8266
E-Mail: info@heartwormsociety.org
www.heartwormsociety.org

### American Holistic Veterinary Medical Association (AHVMA)
P. O. Box 630
Abingdon, MD 21009-0630
Telephone: (410) 569-0795
Fax: (410) 569-2346
E-Mail: office@ahvma.org
www.ahvma.org

### American Veterinary Medical Association (AVMA)
1931 North Meacham Road, Suite 100
Schaumburg, IL 60173-4360
Telephone: (800) 248-2862
Fax: (847) 925-1329
www.avma.org

### ASPCA Animal Poison Control Center
Telephone: (888) 426-4435
www.aspca.org

### British Veterinary Association (BVA)
7 Mansfield Street
London
W1G 9NQ
Telephone: 020 7636 6541
Fax: 020 7908 6349
E-Mail: bvahq@bva.co.uk
www.bva.co.uk

**Canine Eye Registration Foundation (CERF)**
P.O. Box 199
Rantoul, Il 61866-0199
Telephone: (217) 693-4800
Fax: (217) 693-4801
E-Mail: CERF@vmdb.org
www.vmdb.org

**Orthopedic Foundation for Animals (OFA)**
2300 E. Nifong Boulevard
Columbia, MO 65201-3806
Telephone: (573) 442-0418
Fax: (573) 875-5073
E-Mail: ofa@offa.org
www.offa.org

**US Food and Drug Administration Center for Veterinary Medicine (CVM)**
7519 Standish Place
HFV-12
Rockville, MD 20855
Telephone: (240) 276-9300
E-Mail: AskCVM@fda.hhs.gov
www.fda.gov/AnimalVeterinary/

## PUBLICATIONS

### Books

Adamson, Eve. *Complete Guide to a Healthy Dog.* TFH Publications, Inc., 2015.

Leach, Laurie. *The Gifted Puppy Program: 40 Games, Activities, and Exercises to Raise a Brilliant, Happy Dog.* TFH Publications, Inc., 2015.

Libby, Tracy. *High-Energy Dogs.* TFH Publications, Inc., 2009.

Swager, Peggy. *Training the Hard-to-Train Dog.* TFH Publications, Inc., 2009.

### Magazines

**AKC Family Dog**
American Kennel Club
260 Madison Avenue
New York, NY 10016
Telephone: (800) 490-5675
E-Mail: familydog@akc.org
www.akc.org/pubs/familydog

**AKC Gazette : Digital Edition**
American Kennel Club
260 Madison Avenue
New York, NY 10016
www.akc.org/pubs/gazette/digital_edition.cfm

### Websites

**Nylabone**
www.nylabone.com

**TFH Publications, Inc.**
www.tfh.com

# INDEX

Note: Page numbers in **bold** indicate a photograph.

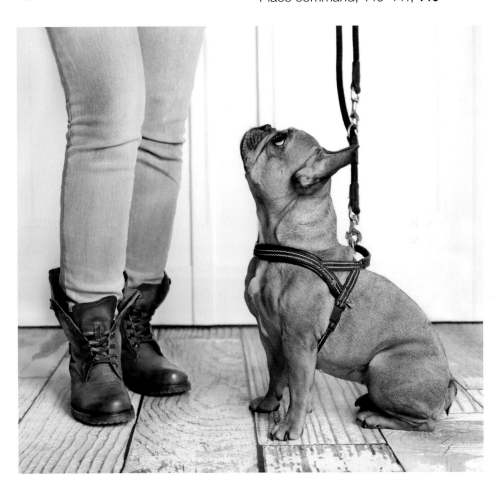

## DEDICATION

For Blazer, the best student I've ever had.

## ABOUT THE AUTHOR

**Janice Biniok** has written numerous articles and books on companion animals. She is a member of the Dog Writers Association of America (DWAA) and has an English degree from the University of Wisconsin-Milwaukee. She has been training and communicating with dogs for more than 35 years, but her five years working in the sport of canine musical freestyle impressed her with the dog's ability to learn an amazing number of human commands. This book is an opportunity for her to help others achieve a higher level of communication with their dogs.

## PHOTOS

Adya (Shutterstock.com): 93, 207; Africa Studio (Shutterstock.com): back cover, 12; Alain Lauga (Shutterstock.com): 165; Alena Ozerova (Shutterstock.com): 58; Andresr (Shutterstock.com): 215; Andriy Solovyov (Shutterstock.com): 38, 235; anetapics (Shutterstock.com): 44, 148; Anke van Wyk (Shutterstock.com): 103 ; Anna Hoychuk (Shutterstock.com): 126; Anna Jagla (Shutterstock.com): 3; Arman Zhenikeyev (Shutterstock.com): 49; Aseph (Shutterstock.com): 217; Barna Tanko (Shutterstock.com): 191; bikeriderlondon (Shutterstock.com): 19; Budimir Jevtic (Shutterstock.com): 116; CBCK (Shutterstock.com): 40; Chendongshan (Shutterstock.com): 159; Csehak Szabolcs (Shutterstock.com): 87; cynoclub (Shutterstock.com): 3, back cover; David Charles Cottam (Shutterstock.com): 48; dezi (Shutterstock.com): 18; dmvphotos (Shutterstock.com): 53; dogboxstudio (Shutterstock.com): 168, 196; dotshock (Shutterstock.com): 123; dwphotos (Shutterstock.com): 214; eClick (Shutterstock.com): 72; Elena Grigorieva (Shutterstock.com): 24; Elena Noeva (Shutterstock.com): 89; Elena Trash (Shutterstock.com): 189; Elya Vatel (Shutterstock.com): 3; Eric Isselee (Shutterstock.com): front cover, 219, 227; Ermolaev Alexander (Shutterstock.com): 239; everst (Shutterstock.com): 122; gorillaimages (Shutterstock.com): 150; gpointstudio (Shutterstock.com): 14; Gunnar Rathbun (Shutterstock.com): 201; Hannamariah (Shutterstock.com): 139; Helen E. Grose (Shutterstock.com): 182; Hitdelight (Shutterstock.com): 8; Inna Astakhova (Shutterstock.com): 192; Jagodka (Shutterstock.com): front cover, 69, 166; Jaromir Chalabala (Shutterstock.com): 31, 76; Javier Brosch (Shutterstock.com): 16, 21, 96, 110, 112, 134, 147, 175, 186, 255; Jenny Sturm (Shutterstock.com): 251; Jeroen van den Broek (Shutterstock.com): 77; Jim Parkin (Shutterstock.com): 198; Jorg Hackemann (Shutterstock.com): 140; Jose Arcos Aguilar (Shutterstock.com): 98; Karen Walker (Shutterstock.com): 146; Kekyalyaynen (Shutterstock.com): 119; Kellymmiller73 (Shutterstock.com): 95; Kenneth William Caleno (Shutterstock.com): 156; Kittibowornphatnon (Shutterstock.com): 161; Ksenia Raykova (Shutterstock.com): 213; Kuznetcov_Konstantin (Shutterstock.com): 247; l i g h t p o e t (Shutterstock.com): 4 (right), 35, 99; leungchopan (Shutterstock.com): 34; Liliya Kulianionak (Shutterstock.com): 94 (left); Lisa Turay (Shutterstock.com): 74; Lunja (Shutterstock.com): 5, 184; MANDY GODBEHEAR (Shutterstock.com): 51, 230; Marcel Jancovic (Shutterstock.com): 62; Marie Dolphin (Shutterstock.com): 46; Mariia Masich (Shutterstock.com): 28; Mark Herreid (Shutterstock.com): 90; Mat Hayward (Shutterstock.com): 32, 175; Matej Kastelic (Shutterstock.com): 64; mdmmikle (Shutterstock.com): 23; mezzotint (Shutterstock.com): 60; Michelle D. Milliman (Shutterstock.com): 205; mikeledray (Shutterstock.com): 223; MilisiArt (Shutterstock.com): 3; Monika Wisniewska (Shutterstock.com): 132; Monkey Business Images (Shutterstock.com): 120, 133; Natalia Fadosova (Shutterstock.com): 42; nenetus (Shutterstock.com): 199; Nina Buday (Shutterstock.com): 241; Odua Images (Shutterstock.com): 25; Olimpik (Shutterstock.com): 84; otsphoto (Shutterstock.com): 194, 202, 211; Paul Leong (Shutterstock.com): 26 (left); Pavel Shlykov (Shutterstock.com): 52; photo_master2000 (Shutterstock.com): 109; Pressmaster (Shutterstock.com): 128, 171; Ratikova (Shutterstock.com): 83; Raywoo (Shutterstock.com): 57; Rita Kochmarjova (Shutterstock.com): 181 Rohappy (Shutterstock.com): 178; Runa Kazakova (Shutterstock.com): 107; Sabrina Hill (Shutterstock.com): 27; Sari Reid (Shutterstock.com): 108; schubbel (Shutterstock.com): 67, 94 (right); Scott Dumas (Shutterstock.com): 163; Sergey Bogdanov (Shutterstock.com): 180; Shanta Giddens (Shutterstock.com): 30; ShutterDivision (Shutterstock.com): 209; siamionau pavel (Shutterstock.com): 100; smikeymikey1 (Shutterstock.com): 4 (left); Soloviova Liudmyla (Shutterstock.com): 26 (right), 80, 137, 155, 172; SpeedKingz (Shutterstock.com): 105, 221; SunyawitPhoto (Shutterstock.com): 81; supercat (Shutterstock.com): 22; Surkov Dimitri (Shutterstock.com): 118; Susan Schmitz (Shutterstock.com): 125, 145; V. J. Matthew (Shutterstock.com): 177; Vivienstock (Shutterstock.com): 121; vvvita (Shutterstock.com): 153; wavebreakmedia (Shutterstock.com): 6, 143; WilleeCole Photography (Shutterstock.com): 37, 73, 111, 114; Yuri Kravchenko (Shutterstock.com): 129; Zuzule (Shutterstock.com): 124